$HADOW
DOLLAR$

$HADOW DOLLAR$

GYPSY FAULS

ISBN: 978-1-7359478-0-8 – Paperback
ISBN: 978-1-7359478-3-9 - Hardcover
eISBN: 978-1-7359478-1-5 - ePub
eISBN: 978-1-7359478-2-2 - mobi

Printed in the United States of America   1 0 2 0 2 0

∞This paper meets the requirements of ANSI/NISO Z39.48-1992 (Permanence of Paper)

CHAPTER ONE

When Attorney General Janet Reno ordered the FBI to cease investigating the federal block grant fraud in Baltimore, no one said a word. When questions were asked about the legality of stopping the inquiry which would have led to many more indictments, no one gave an explanation. It was simply stated that the president did not want the investigation to continue.

But why? There was no logical reason for the Clinton White House not to want the truth told. It was hoped that documenting the abuses would bring about audits in major American cities where federal funds had been diverted.

A review of federal block grant applications indicated that massive amounts of funding had been allocated for many projects in Baltimore City. Although the grantee performance reports indicated most projects had been completed, an inspection of the project locations verified that absolutely no changes had been made to many of the properties scheduled for funding. False statements had been made to Housing and Urban Development and false documents had been submitted frequently. Permits on the local level were irregular and often false.

At first, I thought this was money laundering and that the city was taking federal funds to subsidize budget shortages. It was explained that, in money laundering, the dollars come from an illegal source and are made legal. What was happening was fraud—money was being obtained based on false statements.

Many elected officials in Baltimore City, the State of Maryland, and Washington, DC, were made aware of the misuse of federal funds. I visited offices of Baltimore City councilmen and patiently explained that the Department of Housing and Community Development (DHCD) was falsifying documents reporting expenditures. There was photo documentation to substantiate these reported irregularities, many of which have not been corrected to date.

The blatant falsification of documents submitted to Baltimore City, the State of Maryland, and Housing and Urban Development (HUD) was unfathomable. Even worse was the inexplicable behaviors of employees being paid to review documents and review development in neighborhoods. Not one brick had been laid when a grantee performance report had been submitted stating buildings were under construction on the south side of the

900 block of West Baltimore Street. Then, there was the $100,000 allocation for a park on the north side of the 800 block of Baltimore Street where not a blade of grass or tree was ever planted.

As the list of alleged expenditures grew, it was apparent that some sort of fraud was taking place. It could not be called money laundering because this money was coming from the federal government for a stated purpose on a specific site, and being diverted for another use. According to James Cabezas, chief investigator for the office of the Maryland State prosecutor, this was fraud. The false block grant applications and subsequent false grantee reports were acts of perjury with no statute of limitations. It cannot be stated that the fraud was not brought to the attention of individuals at every level of government . . . and there was photo documentation to back up the allegations of abuse of federal funding and community betrayal. Over time, it became apparent that many elected officials did not want to take a stand on this issue by demanding audits. The grantee performance reports should have been invalidated and triggered investigations into massive fraud.

In Baltimore, all lives mattered, and ethnic diversity in communities was encouraged. At some point, black lives began to matter more than others when it came to federal funding requests and the use of the term minority when monies were awarded based solely on race.

Taking advantage of the equal opportunity movement, women got in on the act, quickly becoming "minority contractors." No one checked to verify whether minorities were actually doing the work. Many roofing contracts were subcontracted to non-minority companies. This was noted when all of the workers putting a roof on the Steuart Hill Elementary School were employees of a subcontractor with not one minority employee.

Cities without a conscience quickly learned that there was money to be made by maintaining stockpiles of vacant properties.

It is popular to call Washington, DC, "The Swamp." Every election, the corruption is lamented, and newly elected officials vow to make a change. Once in office, they become trapped and no longer have the courage to ask the tough questions.

H. L. Mencken, the Sage of Baltimore, classified politicians as "an animal which can sit on a fence and yet keep both ears to the ground." Basically, Mencken's theory was that each citizen makes a difference by keeping his own house in order.

The City of Baltimore requested and received federal funds on an annual basis to stabilize vacant properties. No one checked to ensure these funds were actually being used for the stated purpose.

Washington, DC, does not just monitor housing development across the country, it is also a huge participant in the constant search to provide adequate housing for all income levels while preventing total gentrification. Dr. Ben Carson, secretary of Housing and Urban Development (HUD), has been thoughtful and thoroughly analytical in attempting to get a grip on housing issues. As calls mounted for his resignation early in his term, he appeared to be resolute about bringing housing into compliance with federal guidelines. It will be interesting to see how he reacts to revelations of ongoing corruption throughout the US as cities attempt to continue the funneling of money by falsifying documents.

As DC tries to analyze the reason for recent housing debacles, the Trump administration needs to investigate why the top bids were not accepted and what really caused the chaos. Consulting firms currently being touted as "the best" in DC have tentacles going back to the Clinton administration and a troubled past. Ben Carson and numerous other federal officials should have monitored irregularities. A "watchlist" should exist with additional monitoring of any former DHCD housing officials with any links to the Clinton administration or Clinton Foundation.

The belief that blame for federal funding abuses rests with employees who failed to properly monitor projects is correct to a degree, but what about the systemic abuse of federal funding by a layer of multiethnic individuals whose intent was, and still is, to cash in by skimming funds intended for the less fortunate? The use of a system to award contracts based on race and political connections rather than qualifications should be investigated. Elected officials must be held accountable legally for failing to ensure projects were completed in compliance with contracts.

Representation needs to include accepting responsibility for the physical areas on maps designating official districts. Elected officials need to walk each block, cameras in hand, and note conditions. A plan for improving specific locations which negatively impact public health, safety, and welfare should be implemented within the time frame mandated by law. There should be no exemptions for compliance based on ownership, and court action should be applied in an equitable manner with no exceptions for ownership by government, quasi-public entities, or nonprofits. Nocturnal tours of neighborhoods can also be most enlightening. It is amazing to compare zoning and occupancy to the number of vehicles parked at night. Census takers could readily cross-reference license plates to gain additional information of actual occupancy.

A soft-spoken, legitimate descendant of slaves requested the "$5 Indian" be included in this indictment of monetary abuse based on race. She noted there was no better example of this than Elizabeth Warren, a.k.a. "Pocahontas," who claimed to be Native American, based on being what turned out to be less than 1 percent Native American, to gain preferential treatment including financial aid and scholarships.

Every student in America should be afforded the opportunity to discover our true history. This would include an objective video showing the land currently owned by Native Americans and treaties which exist. It would also include information on incentives created to benefit genuine Native Americans and their descendants. Their information should be readily available to all Americans.

Perhaps there could also be a video on San Jacinto which depicts land previously owned by Mexico and treaties. The San Jacinto Museum of History features an exhibit which details this portion of American history which is not readily taught in schools.

CHAPTER TWO

There have been many successes in the private housing sector in Baltimore. Otis Warren Jr., a prominent minority real estate developer and owner of Otis Warren of Maryland, Inc., properly developed two projects in the western section of the city. It is interesting to note that CHAP, the Commission for Historical and Architectural Preservation, reviewed the Warren developments for historic compliance and denied tax credits for alleged noncompliance of wooden cornice restoration on West Fayette Street while allowing tax credits in the 100 block of South Arlington Avenue, a botched architectural "restoration" completed by a development group from Towson. Warren's development on North Fulton Avenue and 1500 blocks of West Fayette Street have been well maintained for decades. Otis Warren Jr. was the *Baltimore Sun's* 2019 Business and Civic Hall of Fame Honoree.

Dr. Ben Carson has the innate capability to restructure HUD. He will not let the fact that many decaying areas in urban and some rural communities had funding allocated. As a successful surgeon, he was lauded for diagnosing and dealing with rare cranial situations. It does not appear to be his nature to ignore cause and effect. There are those who can recognize or diagnose a problem, but only few with the expertise and creativity to actually correct an issue.

There is little doubt the Trump administration will rebuild slum areas and demand accountability for past funding abuses. Like William Donald Schaefer, the "do it now" mindset is part of how Trump functions. Demanding accountability is inherent in his approach to both life and business success. He will not be tolerant or compliant when funds are requested to do what was allegedly already finished.

Kimberly Klacik embodies the qualities needed to identify and correct gross inequities which exist in some areas of Baltimore City. Her recent video documenting horrific conditions resulting from decades of mismanagement is a brave attempt to finally bring to light what has long been ignored. This articulate young woman can and will challenge Kweisi Mfume for Congress on the real issues.

There is finally a president in the White House who has the courage to stand behind a podium and state the truth.

One does not need to like the manner in which a statement is made to validate the accuracy of the opinion.

It is fascinating to see how Al Sharpton, a snake-oil purveyor of morality, has visited the White House so frequently. This self-appointed spokesperson for the minority community turned his back on those he purported to represent by ignoring obvious abuses in minority neighborhoods throughout America. His blatant greed is evident in the commercial promoting auto loans at a rate of 362 percent interest.

At least with Al Sharpton, you know what you are getting. Anti-white rhetoric is guaranteed to incite tensions even if all the facts are not in.

CHAPTER THREE

When federal efforts were underway to clean up the Chesapeake Bay, Congresswoman Barbara Mikulski noted that the State of Maryland could not exempt itself from compliance. For decades Baltimore City has maintained a discriminatory code enforcement policy. DHCD, nonprofits, and quasi-public entities have routinely been exempted from code compliance while private citizens are prosecuted in a tainted judicial system. Many buildings owned or controlled by government have been allowed to deteriorate to the point of collapse while extreme code compliance has been demanded on nearby privately held properties.

At one point, a proposal was developed which would have allowed a blighted property to be removed from a HUD program and another vacant building substituted. The deteriorated property could be renovated and sold. Code compliance would be achieved and blight eliminated. Bill Tamburrino of HUD was open to the concept. It made no sense for the city to maintain blighted properties and operate a discriminatory code enforcement policy. It was suggested a writ of mandamus be obtained via the courts giving the city six months to develop a plan to renovate or dispose of all vacant properties. It was obvious the federal funds obtained to keep the vacant buildings clean and boarded were not being used properly.

An analysis of Congress would readily identify legislators who have held office for decades and, by their inaction, condoned criminal mismanagement of federal funds. Press coverage of popular causes such as "Save the Bay" enabled legislators to espouse equity in enforcement of environmental regulations to ensure water would be safe for swimming and the spawning of seafood. Congresswoman Barbara Mikulski, always an advocate for the people, demanded compliance by all levels of government and the private sector. It is too bad the same level of compliance was not demanded in neighborhoods where people were drowning emotionally from daily exposure to slum conditions in housing and rampant crime.

Proponents of term limitations for legislators need to be more vocal and insist that legislation be introduced to effect change.

CHAPTER FOUR

Baltimore, Detroit, Newark, and other major cities appear to have been part of a network of corruption. There have been multiple opportunities to identify municipalities and halt the syphoning off of billions of dollars. Simply put, no one had the courage to come forward and demand that federal funds be used for the stated purposes. They continue to call Washington "The Swamp," but I don't believe naïve legislators are prepared for the sellout of their souls. Many have hopes of making a change and are elected based on campaign promises. Imagine the inner conflicts that must develop when funds are diverted.

Governor Hogan recently announced he is going to help Baltimore by tearing down blighted properties. He may not be able to just come in and clear substandard properties, especially those allegedly already renovated with federal funds. In many instances, matching state funds were not properly monitored. This was evidenced when the City of Baltimore submitted inaccurate ownership information to the State of Maryland expecting it to be rubber-stamped. Perhaps this is really an intent to destroy the evidence on the part of some, but, by entering addresses and tax sale information, abuses will be readily documented.

HUD provided funds on an annual basis to secure all vacant properties owned or controlled by DHCD. A drive through so many neighborhoods documents those funds were never used—at least not for the stated purpose. Broken windows, bulging masonry walls, boarded openings, and piled-up trash abounded. It was obvious city, state, and federal employees were not comparing many funding requests to actual sites and verifying completion to actual sites before funds were released.

Most Americans won't drive through "bad neighborhoods" and this is part of the problem. Rather than watching edgy crime shows on TV, why not take a tour of your city and do a reality check? Be prepared to be stared at and possibly stopped by cops who might think you are in the neighborhood to purchase drugs.

At some point the issues of code compliance in public, health, safety, and welfare will come up. Every so often there will be an exposé on substandard housing when a criminal act is associated with the problem. For the most part, many major issues are ignored until it is documented these unsightly conditions have health impacts for peeling lead paint.

CHAPTER FIVE

With the passage of the National Historic Structures Tax Act, there was an influx of homeowners and investors. Imagine being able to renovate income-producing property and write it off in five years. Some buyers were successful in obtaining vacant properties for rehab while others simply could not purchase properties or get permits to renovate. One investor from Washington had purchased property in the 800 block of West Baltimore Street. He was unable to get any cooperation from DHCD. Charles Chadwick had purchased the property in the unit block of South Carey Street which was to become his residence. Mr. Chadwick's parents had magnificently restored a home in the 1400 block of Hollins Street, so it only seemed natural for him to want to renovate a property close by.

The city condemned property on the north side of the 800 block of West Baltimore Street and wanted to obtain federal funds for Section 8 housing. Hearings before several Board of Estimates were heated when the president of the Union Square Local Development Corporation testified in opposition, stating that one day the University of Maryland might want to expand west of Martin Luther King Jr. Boulevard. It made no sense to rezone sections of West Baltimore Street to residential. In one grant application, $100,000 was requested and received for a park on this very same site. On the north side of the 800 block, not one tree was ever planted and there never was a park. Fortunately, the University of Maryland has expanded west of Martin Luther King Jr. Boulevard and development continues to date.

Design and use rival renovated urban areas in San Francisco and Georgetown. In Washington, Congress continues to deal with the domestic deficit most Americans are unaware of. Hopefully, the Trump administration will require every municipality to submit to a financial solvency review prior to turning over any block grant funds. Then, expenditures should be audited and actual work documented before additional money is drawn down on any project.

The news media shares the guilt for select coverage of urban issues. The *Baltimore Sun* papers could and should have demanded accountability from DHCD. It was no secret that the media had an acrimonious relationship with William Donald Schaefer, as Baltimore City councilman, mayor of Baltimore City, governor of the State of Maryland, and comptroller of the State of Maryland. Some in the media focused on Schaefer-bashing rather than doing in-depth investigative reporting. How could these intelligent people drive by slum properties every day and fail to associate addresses with funding request documents? To this day, no one has bothered to develop a master ownership list, funding allocated, and verify completion of projects.

Following the infamous city council hearing on March 7, 1995, where my civil rights were violated, I met with Congressman Ben Cardin on several occasions. He initially seemed impressed by the documentation that existed which supported allegations of fraud. We went over the documents several times and traced the funding allocated, forged permits, and photo documentation showing the work was never done.

It was Congressmen Cardin who contacted a major news network. The investigative reporters who came to Baltimore had spent hours going over documents and photographs to ensure they had total understanding of how the block grant scam had worked.

In the no-bid housing scandal, it was obvious some minority contractors went from state to state, city to city, defrauding federal programs. They formed LLCs or corporations which functioned just long enough to get the money before being declared in default.

Such was the case with Mecca Construction in Baltimore. The corporation had defaulted in New Jersey and Georgia but was still "invited" to come to Baltimore.

There was a time when there was a point of honor in Baltimore. The words of William Donald Schaefer, mayor, and Hyman Pressman, comptroller, were revered and "do it now" meant something would be corrected immediately. Both Schaefer and Pressman took the time to ensure that what they said would happen *did* happen. Schaefer was famous for having his chauffeur alter the route home in order to drive by and check the status of a project. Pressman, as comptroller, monitored the funds. In a way, they were a dream team and worked together from 1963 to 1986.

Pressman demanded accountability from city employees and had the "annoying habit" of calling anyone suspected of wasting time at 8:30 a.m. to see if there was a live body behind the desk to answer the phone. Pressman should have been alive to deal with DHCD employees too lazy or incompetent to verify the accuracy of grantee performance reports. He would never have tolerated the falsification of financial documents by any employee on any level of government.

There was a time when I respected elected officials and thought they wanted the best for the residents of their districts. Respect turned to pity when I saw how so many legislators in the city, state, and federal government remained silent when they became aware of the fraud involving federal funds. One by one, they promised to look into DHCD and do something about the horrendous vacant building problem in Baltimore. Promises were also made regarding code enforcement. To date, renovated properties are not properly maintained and exterior inspections are not done to ensure code compliance.

The Commission for Historical and Architectural Preservation (CHAP) is no longer an independent entity but under the jurisdiction of the Department of Housing and Community Development. The local historic district is the agency responsible for monitoring preservation issues on a daily basis. The failure of CHAP to patrol historic districts to ensure compliance does not excuse the State of Maryland or the National Historic Trust from overseeing compliance in historic districts. Why spend funds to designate historic districts, renovate properties, and often participate in funding projects if basic maintenance is ignored?

When a comprehensive plan was announced to clean up the Chesapeake Bay, there was massive media coverage. Elected officials from every impacted state came on board in support of the project which mandated local, state, and federal compliance. It was Congresswoman Barbara Mikulski's comment that gave inspiration to everyone involved. She pledged compliance on the part of every level of government and emphasized that the federal government was not above the law.

The Union Square Association, Inc.

February 15, 1991

Mr. Ronald Miles
Program Manager
Department of Housing and Community Development
417 East Fayette Street
Baltimore, Maryland 21202

Dear Mr. Miles:

It is my understanding from telephone conversations with you and Sal Mimone that the property at 35 S. Carey Street recently acquired by Charles A. S. Chadwick was included on a list of vacants sent to you by the Hollins Market Neighborhood Association. As a direct result of this communication, Mr. Chadwick received two "5 Day Final Notices" within a two day period issued by two different inspectors and has been scheduled for a hearing with Sal Mimone on 2/19/91.

Mr. Chadwick, who will be our first homeowner on S. Carey Street, acquired his property with the moral assistance of the Union Square Association, Inc., following several housing court trials which resulted not only in guilty verdicts and fines but also in a court order specifying that SERO Property Corporation could not redeem the tax sale certificate on the property. The community has sought code compliance on this property since 1985 in addition to other vacants in the area. Mr. Chadwick was advised he would have to obtain necessary building permits after obtaining CHAP approval for exterior changes, and is in the process of doing the same; he was unaware a permit was needed to put on a new roof which was completed in two segments. Mr. Lawrence Chester of Building Inspection is being asked to meet with the owner regarding all necessary permits. A search is underway for the deed to the property which appears to have been misplaced. Understandably, Mr. Chadwick has been reluctant to expend additional monies until he has a deed.

Obviously, it is in the best interest of the City, the community, and DHCD to work with these "pioneer spirits" still willing to attempt to convert slum properties into homes using private funds. To this end, I am requesting that Mr. Chadwick be extended all courtesies and offered whatever assistance is available. He is an extremely concentious young professional deemed to be an asset to the community; however, like most citizens, he becomes frustrated when the system works unfairly. We cannot afford to discourage others like him.

As you are aware, there has been an on-going vacant building research project in our area since 1985 when a list of vacants needing immediate attention was developed which was sent to Mr. John Huppert. The list sent by The Hollins Market Neighborhood Association, as reviewed by telephone, appears not to be comprehensive. I have asked Rita McCurley of COIL, Inc., to send you a copy of the 1985 list with updated notations. It is my inderstanding the following addresses were forwarded to Sal Mimone by your office:

S. Calhoun Street	- 17, 116	Pratt Street-	924,1134,1136,1226
Carlton Street	- 37, 104,106,108,110,112	Hollins St. -	1001,1009,1011,
Carrollton Ave.	- 127		1017,1319
Lombard Street	- 1036,1120,1122,1124,1143	Stockton St.-	42,44,46,48,114,
Schroeder Street	- 36,44		116,118,120
Carey Street	- 15,17,20,22,28,30,31,33,35		

P.O. Box 20520, Baltimore, Maryland 21223   (301) 472-2663

There are numerous other vacants in the area, some of which are owned by the Mayor and City Council. It is my understanding that the list you received did include some properties owned by the City; however, these properties were not forwarded to Mr. Mimone requesting immediate action. Bernard Murphy, Director of Legislative Reference, has advised us that the City is bound by the housing code and is subject to the same enforcement procedures and penalties as private owners. Therefore, violation notices should be issued immediately on all vacant deteriorating properties. It may be necessary to ask that an independent prosecutor be appointed to handle all cases involving M&CC owned structures.

To ensure equity in code enforcement, a comprehensive list of vacants is being forwarded to your office for referral to appropriate area offices. Mr. Mimone is aware that some privately owned properties and M&CC owned properties requiring immediate attention were not included in the initial list which included the Chadwick structure.

It is my sincere hope that City Council Bill 1230 will assist in resolving the vacant building dilema in our section of the city. Your presence at the hearing would be appreciated. Please call me at 945-3153 or leave a message with Rita McCurley at COIL, Inc., 837-2036, if additional information is needed.

Thanking you for your assistance, I remain

Sincerely yours,

Legislative Liason, The Union Square Association, Inc., on Loan to COIL, Inc.

cc: Honorable Kurt Schmoke, Mayor
     Honorable Joseph DiBlasi
     Honorable Edward Reisinger
     Honorable Timothy Murphy
     Bernard Murphy
     Charles A.S. Chadwick
     CHAP
     Hollins Market Neighborhood Association
     file

CHAPTER SIX

In Baltimore City, corruption was rampant in code enforcement. The city exempted properties owned or controlled by the city from compliance. Quasi-public entities and many nonprofits were exempted. It was not uncommon for individual property owners to face court compliance hearings when dilapidated or vacant properties located nearby remained in slum condition.

The Union Square Association filed a case hoping the court would order CHAP and the city to comply with housing laws. The case was never heard because it could not be documented that it was the imperative duty of CHAP to enforce its ordinance. The Baltimore City State Attorney's Office refused to turn over documents from a precedent-setting case in Leakin Park.

Hundreds of structures are being demolished, creating vacant lots for development. The construction materials are supposedly being recycled, but nowhere is there any documentation of the disposition of funds obtained to rehab these very same structures. Fortunately, the technology exists to compile and compare a list of properties demolished to addresses in federal block grant applications stating buildings would be renovated. Little has been said by HUD about the massive funding abuses by many American cities, but that does not mean the agency is not aware of the massive fraud that went on for decades.

It would be good if the Trump administration did an evaluation on the financial stability of every locale requesting federal funds. Elected officials should also be held accountable for failure to ensure that funds were used for the stated purpose and for not insisting that a massive investigation take place to determine what happened to the money.

Perhaps a utopian scenario could be put in place, giving every recipient of federal funds the opportunity to request amnesty for past abuse in exchange for coming clean and documenting what issues led to the movement of funds from the intended use. There should be no amnesty if the funds cannot be accounted for and future funding should be allocated on a probationary status with monthly reviews of the local government's fiscal stability.

It seems there would be laws governing the submission of false documents to government agencies which would be enforced. The applications for funding were falsified. The grantee performance reports to HUD were falsified.

The inspection reports to DHCD showing completion were falsified. When all of this was reported, no one took action.

The office of the Maryland State prosecutor stated it was not within their jurisdiction. Individual elected officials could and should have acted to bring an end to funding abuses but simply did not have the courage to take on the corrupt system which has been in place for decades. The political ecosystem created a swamp where disingenuous representatives could thrive to the detriment of all Americans—not just Baltimoreans! The concept of draining the swamp sounds good, but it would make more sense to get rid of the flesh-eating bacteria in the swamp rather than release the disease back into society. It would only take a few months, perhaps six, to diagnose the level of corruption and initiate the removal of elected officials who failed to cooperate.

When I received a call from the FBI stating they wanted to meet with me regarding the status of the investigation, I was pleased. I certainly did not anticipate the outcome of the meeting. When I was told the inspector general's office had told the FBI to drop the investigation into fraud in Baltimore City, I was dumbfounded. My first question was, why? I was told the Justice Department had ordered the investigation to be halted on orders from the White House. I was outraged and wanted to know how something like this could happen in America when we had separation of powers.

James Cabezas, chief investigator for the Maryland State prosecutor's office, was aware of some details of my relationship with investigators. I asked Jim if there was anything his office could do, since crimes had clearly been committed involving falsification of documents and funding reports. For some reason, I thought the State of Maryland might care. James Cabezas said, at the least, anyone with knowledge of the falsification could be charged with perjury.

If only H. L. Mencken had been alive! Writers at the *Baltimore Sun* seemed not to care about investigating the massive fraud involving every level of government in Maryland.

The City of Baltimore has exempted the Housing Authority of Baltimore City (HABC) from compliance with building codes and other regulations. Numerous properties owned by HABC and other quasi-public entities are not registered as a rental property as required by law. 100 South Mount Street is one such property. A list of Section 8 rental properties is not readily available from the city and FOIA, freedom of information, requests have to be filed to gain access to documents.

The current list of real estate for sale in Baltimore needs some advertising help—perhaps Smith Barney could add a novel approach. A good start would be to get a photograph online for each property available with an asking price. Why aren't photographs available? Once again, there is a less than enthusiastic handling of marketing. Who, if anyone, is actually monitoring this site for quality control?

Obtaining ownership information for properties in Baltimore City can be a challenge. This is especially true if the property was ever in a tax sale or was included in a funding request. The emphasis clearly was on getting money while frequently violating the constitutional rights of private owners. There were instances when addresses were listed on applications for federal and state funding for acquisition and rehabilitation without the knowledge of the owners.

My phone rang nonstop the afternoon it was discovered that the home of Sterling Stanfield, who resided in the unit block of South Arlington Avenue, had been included in a grant request. The property, along with several others, was located in the Union Square National Register Area, the local historic district, and the Poppleton urban renewal area. Within hours, state and local legislators received ample documentation from residents opposing the illegal inclusion of the Stanfield residence. The masterminds of the HUD scam had really screwed up. Sterling Stanfield

was a minority homeowner and a successful street businessman who controlled a large area of Baltimore. I was
told it took "real balls" for a municipal employee to be so
stupid. It was inconceivable that the privately owned residence of an American citizen could be included in a funding request for developers without his knowledge. My relationship with DHCD became even more venomous
when I undertook the task of matching up addresses on
the funding applications, ownership documentation, and
grantee performance reports.

There was a time when I could walk into the permit
division of DHCD and request a copy of all permits issued
on a specific address. For several months, municipal
employees readily provided this public information,
knowing of my interest in code compliance. Then, access
became more difficult, especially when the properties
were located in urban renewal areas or controlled by local
government. After the embarrassing Stanfield fiasco, there
was an unwritten declaration of war—the cost of copies
rose to twenty dollars per page, where it remains to this
day. Fortunately, there were several municipal employees
who discreetly made documents available, believing in the
cause. I will be forever indebted to these employees who
jeopardized their jobs in the interest of Baltimore.

Hopefully, the Trump administration will do an in-
depth audit of major American cities prior to just handing

out money for the rehabilitation of properties. Such an audit should include photo documentation of properties which could be cross-referenced to past funding applications. The rush to demolish entire blocks of dilapidated structures in urban areas cannot be ignored, especially when these properties were slated for renovation in prior funding requests and false granting performance reports were filed.

CITY OF BALTIMORE

WILLIAM DONALD SCHAEFER, Mayor

NEIGHBORHOOD PROGRESS
ADMINISTRATION/DHCD

MARION W. PINES, Commissioner
222 East Saratoga Street, Baltimore, Maryland 21202

December 11, 1986

The Honorable Donald Hammen
Chairman, Urban Affairs Committee
Baltimore City Council
550 City Hall
100 Holliday Street
Baltimore, Maryland 21202

Dear Councilman Hammen:

Pursuant to your request to review our process for disposition of City-owned
land, I discussed with staff our historic as well as our present policy for
disposition.

Please let me assure you that it is the policy of NPA/DHCD to advertise
City-owned property before disposition. As always, there have been occas-
sional exceptions to the rule, but they are few and far between. As this
discussion relates to our actions in the Poppleton area, I will reiterate
our position that, before disposing of land or property, our staff will
inform the Poppleton Briefing Group and will advertise in the local press.

I am hopeful that this letter to you, as Chairman of the Urban Affairs
Committee, will provide you the necessary assurances.

It has been a pleasure working with you in successfully resolving the issues
raised during the amendment process.

Sincerely,

Marion W. Pines
Commissioner

MWP/MS:apc

A PARTNERSHIP OF HOUSING, COMMUNITY DEVELOPMENT AND MANPOWER RESOURCES

CHAPTER SEVEN

A fire on South Carey Street was the proverbial last straw—eight people had died, five of them children. There had been complaints of overcrowding and excessive noise at this rental property, which had single-family zoning. There were a total of twenty-one residents. Newspaper accounts following the fire indicated the property was being used for two dwelling units. Residents had stated three families occupied the property, which had subsidized rentals. There was no way this property should not have been issued violation notices prior to the fire. And three families could not have legally been approved for occupancy.

In the 1000 block of Booth Street, there was more evidence of fraud involving subsidized rentals. A man routinely met a postal employee on the north side of the street across from a vacant Section 8 rental in dilapidated condition to pick up a check. The house was not habitable, no windows, no electric, but yet, a Section 8 check was being delivered to someone who allegedly lived in that property on a corner.

On South Carey Street a sidewalk car wash business flourished, being operated from a vacant DHCD property with a very active water account.

The Eckenrode Building on North Carrollton Avenue, located behind the dime store, which had been condemned for urban renewal purposes, housed a major dogfighting operation. For months, dogs could be seen headed for what may have been their last fight. The newspapers would print stories about dogs being kept illegally in buildings without proper licenses, but not one story about the organized dogfighting ring.

The state attorney office finally got involved after a dog was found dead in the alley. But there was no media coverage—no one wanted to acknowledge the prevalence and acceptance of dogfighting in the black community. It was hidden like cockfighting in the South. The close relationship between some employees in the state attorney office and operators of the dogfights was noted at a groundbreaking on West Baltimore Street. I was amazed when an assistant state attorney greeted the K9 entrepreneurs and slapped them on the back as they chatted for several minutes. It was like those who knew this allowed it to go on for decades, as it did in many areas, until there was a celebrity target like Michael Vick.

Some athletes in the US pay a higher price than others

when it comes to violating the social conscience of America. Pity the athlete who is tackled by PETA.

The Irish Railroad Workers Museum headquartered at 918 Lemon Street, across from the B&O Railroad Museum, was the brainchild of Judge Thomas H. Ward of Bolton Hill.

The Wards, Tom and Joyce, had befriended us early on when we were founding the Union Square Association. Tom became a mentor, encouraging us to draw families to the Union Square area to strengthen the viability of the community. We had the pleasure of visiting the Wards at their retreat on the Cheat River in West Virginia, where a railroad car validated Tom's enthusiasm for everything B&O. It was Judge Ward who encouraged me to do whatever was necessary to block the demolition of the houses in the 900 block of Lemon Street and worry about the consequences later.

During the riots, when our neighbors were so frightened about looting and fires being set on West Baltimore Street, I called Judge Ward for ideas on how to protect our lives and homes. He suggested a bucket brigade system for each block which consisted of a five-gallon bucket of water and blankets in the front room of each house between the windows, which could be used to put out Molotov cocktails that might be hurled through windows. He offered to loan me a gun, which I drove to Bolton Hill to pick up. On the way back to Union Square, I was stopped by a National Guard soldier—thank God they finally arrived—who advised me of my curfew violation but allowed me to continue home, unaware of the loaded gun under my seat.

Battle lines were drawn very quickly when the Department of Housing and Community Development refused to recognize the protected status of structures within the local and National Historic districts.

The 900 block of Lemon Street was included in several different funding requests, and several grantee performance reports. No work was done on the properties which were historically significant. Dan Henson, DHCD commissioner, was aware of the research into funding abuse being done and decided to get rid of the evidence by bulldozing these properties, which had been inhabited by Irishmen who fled Ireland during the potato famine. Fortunately, the streets were too narrow for the demolition equipment, sent out by Hanson during the standoff with preservationists. There was not much media coverage, but seeing live bodies standing on scaffolding erected by renovators, daring the city to proceed with destroying these properties, was amazing.

It wasn't enough to want to save historic properties— there had to be a plan for reuse.

The Mark Steven Show, on Morgan State radio station,

contained a dissertation on Detroit, Newark, and Baltimore urban housing issues. There was a biased presentation of facts with absolutely no in-depth knowledge of what really happened to the millions, even billions, of dollars in federal funding allocated to communities under the block grant programs.

The phrase "black lives matter" may have taken on a totally new meaning in recent years. Black lives have always mattered when it came to counting heads based on race to access federal funds. And, yes, some of those lives have been disrespected for decades. Disrespected, not by any specific group other than the greedy corrupt individuals of any race who knowingly applied for or diverted funding intended to help those in need.

For decades, some minority contractors have ripped off the system for their personal gain. Washington is in a state of panic now because Trump is a businessman who can and will hold local jurisdictions and leaders responsible for federal funds.

CHAPTER EIGHT

Baltimore will be scrutinized in the 2020 election. The battle between Kweisi Mfume, former congressman from Baltimore who also served as president of the National Association for the Advancement of Colored People (NAACP) from 1996 to 2004, and Kimberly Klacik should be of interest. Mfume won the primary in 1986 by a mere two votes. On election eve, I left the celebration for William Donald Schaefer early to convey best wishes from Shaefer to Mfume at the Belvedere Hotel. The infamous celebrity taxi driver from Section 4 in Memorial Stadium was the designated chauffeur. It was a fascinating and fun taxi ride. When I arrived, I entered the room where Mfume's reception was being held. It was almost like the River Jordan parting as a line opened for me to walk through in a predominantly minority crowd. Mfume approached me with misty eyes and thanked me for helping him win the primary. As he took my hands in his, we both knew he had won the primary because of the votes which came from residents of Union Square and other progressive sixth-district thinkers. Mfume had pledged to represent all residents of the area. He was responsive to most community issues but did nothing to end the corruption involving Housing and Urban Development monies. One has to wonder if another term in Congress would be productive, since Mfume did not lead the fight to ensure Baltimore complied with federal guidelines the last time he represented the area as an elected official. Kimberly Klacik has certainly taken on the issues. Perhaps there needs to be an evaluation of the NAACP and its relevance to society as a whole before it moves its headquarters to Washington, DC.

One of the federal block grant abuses involved several properties in the 1000 block of West Fayette Street which were to have been developed by Morning Star Baptist Church for much-needed housing. I can recall standing on West Fayette Street discussing the failure of oversight in the federal program as we looked at the properties, many of which are still in slum condition today. Elijah Cummings, a prominent community leader, also took no action to correct the abuses.

There never was a satisfactory answer to one basic question: what happened to the money? There were numerous properties in the area which were included in more than one funding request. Some properties received state funds, also making the State of Maryland culpable for failure to monitor allocated funding.

There was an annual infamous Board of Estimates meeting in Baltimore where funding was moved from one account to another. Attending the Board of Estimates meetings was essential in following the money trail in Baltimore and, of course, going to the physical location where funds were allegedly spent to verify what had actually been done. The entire urban renewal process was absurd. The media lauded completion of high-profile projects but did no in-depth analysis of what was not being done. The high rollers in this crooked card game were Department of Housing and Community Development and corrupt officials. Money was moved or transferred from one account to another with absolutely no verification of the status of the original request.

Legislators received improper notification, just a list of accounts being transferred with no description shortly before the hearing. There was also no time allotted for review by legislators prior to the hearing. The system was broken for decades, like the promises made to Baltimoreans.

One of the most well-attended community meetings ever held was at Fourteen Holy Martyrs Church.

It was amazing to see how many public officials attended the meeting. The program was entitled, "The Best and Worst of Baltimore Street." We acknowledged the problems and discussed them. West Baltimore Street—to be politically correct, Southwest Baltimore—was on the move. Thanks to Mayor William Donald Schaefer, many of our dreams were becoming reality. He gave us the freedom to find qualified contractors who brought in bids much lower than estimates given by the Department of Housing and Community Development. Arthur Littlepage became a true champion as he represented the West Baltimore Street Merchants Association. We went from brick manufacturer to manufacturer and from contractor to contractor, getting samples of pavers, mortar, and lighting. Yes, Schaefer let us get bids on period street lighting. After all, we were restoring the street that bears the city's name. Our biggest success was getting the north and south sides of West Baltimore Street from Schroeder Street to Fulton Avenue in the national register area and local historic district, much to the disdain of some

DHCD employees who wanted to load the commercially zoned area with Section 8 housing.

M. J. Brody, from the Housing Commission, was absolutely brilliant. He understood urban development and wanted community input. On a walking tour of the Hollins Market Area, both Schaefer and Brody listened intently as we described the Shopsteading program, which would allow developers of income-producing properties to obtain the building for one hundred dollars and write the rehab cost off over a period of five years under a National Historical Structure Tax Act. It was such an honor when a representative of Senator Strom Thurmond came to my home on Union Square to get details of how these programs were envisioned. The next thing I knew, a bill was being introduced into Congress which, if passed, would have a nationwide impact and lead to the redevelopment of decaying urban commercial areas nationwide. And pass it did! One of the proudest moments of my life was when I received the call from William Donald Schaefer stating, "Well, child, we did it," after the bill passed. Schaefer frequently called me "child," which was a nickname he had for me.

Schaefer lost no time in making Baltimore, Maryland, a premier example of urban development. Throughout the city, there was a dramatic transformation from abandoned to occupied with creative uses.

April 16, 1975

Honorable William Donald Schaefer
Mayor, City of Baltimore
City Hall
131 East Redwood Street
Baltimore, Maryland 21201

Dear Mayor Schaefer:

This letter is to advise you of the progress to date regarding the Hollins Market. Contributions have been received for over 80% of the Lexan windows to be installed on the second floor of the brick addition to the market which was built in 1864. The Union Square Association has selected the Hollins Market as its Preservation Week Project and will be coordinating the installation. I met with Mr. Ed Opel to obtain specifications for the work and was also advised that the estimated value of the work was $13,000.00. His office has been most helpful.

We have looked more closely into the Hollins Market being designated as a federal landmark in order that federal funds might be available to aid in the rehabilitation of the market.

I have been asked by Miss Nancy Miller of the Maryland Historical Trust to request that you send her a letter reiterating your support as stated during the tour of the market that Hollins Market obtain Federal Historic Landmark Designation in order to obtain funds. It is very important for the progress that you forward such a letter to Miss Miller. I hope the letter can be written in the near future and would appreciate receiving a copy. I think it makes much more sense to place the Hollins Market, the least altered of the market buildings and a neighborhood amenity, on the Federal Landmark List rather than the market system.

The question of landmark designation and the saving and preservation of the market was raised by me at a meeting of the Baltimore City Committee of the Maryland Historical Trust held on April 9, 1975. I am pleased to say that the committee enthusiastically endorsed the proposal. The committee also recommended that a procedure be instituted for obtaining State funds for the rehabilitation. This can be initiated through the Maryland Historical Trust Annapolis Office. I would be most happy to assist in obtaining the necessary information but feel the City should initiate the procedure. Should additional information be needed please contact me.

2.

The neighborhood is very pleased with the plans for Phase I of the market rehabilitation. The ultimate result will be continued growth of the area and restoration of commercial and residential structures using private funds with the market and Union Square providing the incentive.

I do hope you will be able to step by on Sunday, May 11, to see the community working on the market. I would be especially pleased if you could thank the professional glazier who is installing the windows at no cost to the community once the frames have been prepared and materials supplied.

I am attaching some historical information which you should find interesting. That old "chicken coop" or "shed" turned out to be the original market!

Thank you for your continuing interest and support.

Sincerely,

P.S. You're quite a preservationist even if the road foes wo admit it!

SHOPSTEADING

1887.

To the Public in general.

BALTIMORE, January 1st.

WE have concluded on and after this date, to do a strictly CASH BUSINESS, and, in justice to our many friends and the public in general, we thought it best to explain our reasons. The advantages of the cash plan are so many and so obvious that it has great attractions for all who are in a position to give it a trial; the tendency in that direction is very noticeable. Its benefits are by no means confined to the storekeeper. The saving of money and of the worry and annoyance of the credit system are as much in favor of the consumer as of the dealer, and are so apparent as to make it reasonably clear that the cash system must, before many years, be generally adopted. The drift of business sentiment, and all the changes in business methods, are in the direction of the cash plan. Any one that gives credit is compelled to have two prices, viz:—one price to the cash buyer and another to the credit buyer. An intelligent buyer knows that money is worth interest. If there was nothing to be gained by paying cash for goods no one of good credit would ever consent to do so; it would pay to buy on credit and let the money be invested at interest. The cash buyer pays cash to get a discount, and undoubtedly he does get it, the credit purchaser takes chances and so does the merchant. It is a business of uncertainty. The goods have to be paid for. The customer may trifle, the merchant cannot, we have to pay for goods the same as consumers: they who pay cash get a reasonable discount, and that discount to some is a fair profit. It is to us; if we pay cash for every thing we buy that allows us a discount of from five to seven per cent., and by doing a large business five to seven per cent. profit is a good income. By doing a cash business we can almost sell goods at first cost, or manufacturers' prices, and make a fair profit. It stands to reason, that parties who do a credit business and want to make a profit have to charge from ten to twenty per cent. higher for their goods. And all this comes out of the consumer. We tell you this because it is to your interest as well as ours. We will have but *one price* and that will be the *lowest price* the goods can be sold for, and that is for everybody. It is a cash price which insures to every buyer the very best return for the money invested. We will not put on an extra profit to pay for bad debts, or other expenses incident to a credit business. Buyers are going where they can get the best values, and upon this principle we intend to sell— that is, strictly for cash. It will be to the interest of all to compare our prices with those of others.

Thanking friends for past favors and desiring a continuance of the same, I remain

Respectfully,

W. F. HENDRICKSON,
Dealer in

Millinery, Fancy Goods and Notions,

1429 W. BALTIMORE STREET,

4th door East of Stricker St.

West Baltimore Commercial Area

West Baltimore Street was Baltimore's first major access road to the west, connecting the town with the commercially important Frederick Road. The properties fronting Baltimore Street were easily accessible for suburban development long before much of the remainder of the Union Square area. Many of the area's oldest buildings are concentrated along this route. Because of the heavy traffic along Baltimore Street, it also became the area's commercial center providing all the essentials of nineteenth century living. The corridor currently presents an ideal setting for the restoration of a small segment of Baltimore's nineteenth century commercial character.

In the late eighteenth century the Baltimore Street area contained the country estates of Baltimore's elite. Among those who maintained estates here were William Lorman, an active patriot in the Battle of Baltimore, a wealthy merchant, and a member of City Council; George T. Dunbar, a member of the Maryland Melitia, a banker, and the donor of the land for Hollins Market; William Pinkney, eminent lawyer, Attorney General of Maryland and the United States, a State Senator, member of Congress, Minister to Russia, and a United States Senator from Maryland; and Thorogood Smith, Baltimore's second mayor. Baltimore Street, the area's first road, was the main entrance into the City from the west, linking the estates and giving access to Frederick Road.

As early as 1820 the bucolic retreat of the "Western Precincts" was challenged by the establishment of a steam engine factory and grist mill. Located on Baltimore Street between Schroeder Street and Carrollton Avenue, they both took advantage of Chatsworth Run, the stream which formerly ran near the present bed of Schroeder Street. As early as 1823 a community of working men's residences had been erected here.

Following in guide succession in the 1830's and 40's, the Mount Clare yards of the Baltimore and Ohio Railroad, the locomotive works of Ross Winans, the iron works of Haywood and Barlett, and the Newman Brothers piano factory established major plants, employing thousands, in the open area to the southeast. Residences, and the institutions to support them, quickly rose to house the owners and workers of the factories.

The creation of Union Square in 1847 signaled the arrival of consciously styled suburban development. Development generally occurred in a leap-frog, random fashion, with the Square as the only attempt at rational planning. The businesses of the community were becoming concentrated along Baltimore Street, which handled most of the area's traffic. As the large scale developer finished off the side streets with residential rows in the 1870's and 80's, Baltimore Street became increasingly commercial and many of the first story facades fronting the road were converted into shops.

The types of nineteenth century businesses ensconced along Baltimore Street included a barber shop, drug store, tin shop, bakery, tailor, bowling alley, and a variety of shops catering to the horse and buggy.

By 1890, the process of filling in the grid of streets was virtually complete and the area looked much as it does today. Generally, the finest residences were built on the east-west streets, lesser residences on the north-south streets, and modest residences for laborers and domestics, who were generally black, on the alley streets. In short, the Union Square-Baltimore Street area was a representative slice of a self-contained Baltimore urban village, containing a remarkable diversity and concentration of residential and commercial structures from all architectural periods of the nineteenth and early twentieth century commercial building forms. A relatively complete historical and architectural record, from about the year 1820, remains.

The neighborhood suffered a physical decline after World War II. Interest in the renovation of the Union Square-Baltimore Street-Hollins Market area began approximately ten years ago and should prove to be a significant contribution to the preservation of Baltimore's unique historic and architectural heritage.

Since 1972 the West Baltimore Street Merchants Association has worked with the community to revitalize the commercial corridor and endorsed the expansion of the Union Square Historic and Architectural Preservation District. One major problem had to be resolved--how to treat the vacant commercial structures which had become such an eyesore. It should be noted that some lovely shops, such as those adjacent to Tenser's Shoes and Littlepage's Corner Buildings, are merely covered until development begins.

It was during a tour of the Hollins Market in 1975 that Mayor William Donald Schaefer decided to save the original Hollins Market, the wooden structure behind the 1864 brick meeting hall, and conceived shopsteading as a solution to the vacant buildings in the area and Baltimore City. No one knew when the idea would become reality but it had merit.

The expansion of the Poppleton Urban Renewal boundaries which split the commercial district and created an inequity for merchants west of Carey Street was the catalyst for implementing shopsteading. The Union Square Local Development Corporation, 25 residents and merchants whose names are available upon request, was formed in 1976 to assist shopsteaders and provide services to established merchants. The LDC made a committment in and out of Poppleton.

Many agencies should be thanked for assisting in preparing for shopsteading which is another first for Baltimore and for the nation. The merchants who stayed, indicating that Baltimore Street is viable and who made a committment to preserve the architectural character of the corridor which bears the City's name, deserve much credit. Most of all, it is Mayor William Donald Schaefer who should be thanked for being creative and believing in the future of this area and all of Baltimore.

1316 West Baltimore Street

This structure was built about 1840. Around 1860 the City of
Baltimore banned any roof, including gabled roofs, which allowed
water run-off toward the front of a building. The gabled roof
indicates that the structure was built before this time. The
storefront, a later addition, is composed of cast iron and pressed
sheet metal, popular toward the end of the last century. These
elements, including a recessed entranceway and a decorative cornice should be used in the rehabilitation of the structure to recreate a nineteenth century appearance.

1318 West Baltimore Street

Dating from about 1865, this building was part of the earlier
residential development of the Union Square area. The storefront
was a twentieth century addition. By the end of World War II
essentially all the buildings fronting on Baltimore Street in
this area had been converted to at least partial commercial use.
To preserve the 19th century character of the building, the rehabilitation should include the restoration of the cornice and
two-over-two windows.

1408 West Baltimore Street

Built about 1865, the most outstanding feature of this building
is its elaborate wooden cornice with four large brackets. The
ornate wooden details are features which help to date the period
of construction of the building. The first floor storefront, with
a recessed entranceway, appears to be a twentieth century addition
and can be used to restore the commercial flavor of Baltimore Street.

1410 West Baltimore Street

Built about 1890, the building proudly displays a projecting storefront with elaborate wooden scrollwork. The store window and the
recessed entrance should be used in the restoration of the commercial
character of the building. The similarity of the roof and storefront
cornices indicates that a shop was incorporated into the building's
original designs. The shop housed a barber shop near the turn of the
century. Other features which should be included in a restoration
are the pressed sheet metal decorations with two Union Jack designs
along the roof, and the marble lintels and sills of the windows.

1412 West Baltimore Street

Built about 1825, this is one of the oldest buildings in the area.
Several houses, such as this one, were built along Baltimore Street
out to Frederick Avenue during the early nineteenth century. These
buildings probably housed artisans who set up shops on the first
floor to sell their wares to the many travelers along this route.
The architecturally significant features worth preserving include

the dormer in the gabled, tin roof, the shuttered windows, and the small sallyport, which are all original features.

1432 West Baltimore Street

Built about 1850, this structure was among the first wave of suburban residential development in the area. The storefront cornice which is similar to the roof cornice, with brackets and jigsaw details, indicates that a shop may have been part of the original building designs, or that it was added soon after. These cornices are part of the building's character and should be indicated in the rehabilitation.

1436 West Baltimore Street

The buildings located at the intersections along Baltimore Street were probably among the first to house businesses in the Union Square area. 1436 has been used commercially at least since the turn of the century when it housed a drug store. The building, was constructed about 1850, for residential use, but storefronts were later added to the corner and side. The decorative cornice along the front and side is a necessary part of the building's restoration.

1501 West Baltimore Street

An ice cream shop has been located in this building for over seventy years. In the old days the ice cream was manufactured in the back building along the alley. The building was constructed around 1870. The size indicates that it was probably built for commercial uses. The cornice and the side gallery are nineteenth century elements which will enhance the building's restored appearance.

1502 West Baltimore Street

The building displays fancifully decorated cornices at the roof and above the storefront, and brackets above the second story windows. The storefront includes a divided transom, an old architectural feature. All these details appear to be of the same period, about 1845, indicating that a shop was part of the building's original purpose. These elements are essential parts of recreating the building's original decorative appearance.

1504 West Baltimore Street

Built around 1820, this is one of the oldest extant buildings in the Union Square area. When constructed it was surrounded only by the vast acreage of a few country estates. The removal of its formstone and asphalt would reveal a wooden building, one of the very few of this period left in Baltimore. The structure probably housed some type of artisan and his shop. In its very early days the business would have been supported by the many travelers along Baltimore Street, the access road to the main highway from Baltimore to Frederick.

1506 West Baltimore Street

Built about 1850, the building is decorated with bracketed wooden cornices at the roof and above the storefront. This suggests that a first story shop may have been part of the building's original plans. These elements and the actual storefront, with a recessed entranceway, are typical features of a nineteenth century shop.

1508, 1510 West Baltimore Street

These structures were built as a set about 1865. Though both presently have first floor storefronts, they were probably designed as residences. The existing storefronts, were added later in the nineteenth century. 1508, was used as a Chinese laundry in the early twentieth century.

The conversion of the ground floors into shops represents the growing commercialism of West Baltimore Street at the end of the last century. The wooden store windows, transoms and cornices should be preserved rather than restoring the structures to their original residential appearance.

1512 West Baltimore Street

This structure was constructed as part of a set of two buildings. The trend of constructing homes in pairs was part of the large scale residential development in the area after the Civil War. The growing railroad and iron industries located nearby, created the demand for a local working population.

The bracketed cornices of the roof and the double-arched lintels are part of the building's original designs. These elements, along with the bracketed storefront cornice, added later, will contribute to the building's restored character.

1511 West Baltimore Street

This building has the distinctive mansard roof, a design element of the Second Empire style, which was popular throughout the United States from 1865-1889. The representation of this style on West Baltimore Street attests to the remarkable diversity of architectural styles from all periods of the nineteenth century extant in the Union Square area. The mansard roof, the window patterns of the second and third stories, the cornices and storefront are features which should be preserved to maintain the building's distinct design.

1521 West Baltimore Street

This large four story structure was constructed as one of a set of two buildings. It was probably built as a residence about 1860, in an area of residential and commercial structures. This pattern of development accurately reflects the economic, social and racial heterogeneity which characterized Baltimore's neighborhood villages before the advent of motor transportation.

The cornice and transoms of the storefront appear to have been
added later, but are part of the building's nineteenth century
heritage.

1529 West Baltimore Street

This structure is similar in design to 1521 but is a story shorter.
It too was built about 1860. The pressed sheet metal cornice and
cast iron end brackets of the storefront indicate that the building
was converted for commercial use at the end of the nineteenth century. These features and the transoms of the storefront can help
recreate the commercial appearance characteristic of West Baltimore
Street in the last century.

1625 Frederick Avenue

An electrical repair shop has been located at 1625 for over fifty
years. The building itself dates from about 1840, the gabled roof
suggesting the building's age. Notice that the front facade conforms to the angle of Frederick Avenue, but the side walk retain the
north-south pattern of Baltimore Street. The simple cornice of the
roof and the nine-over-nine windows are remnants of the building's
original details and should be retained in its restoration.

Implementation / Gihon

UNION SQUARE . . . . .

a park

blocks of Victorian rowhouses

the Hollins Market

an historic preservation district

a shopsteading community

a community spirit

. . . . . a living neighborhood

Like the city of which it is a part, Union Square is rich in history and diversity, and it is in the midst of a renaissance.

The Union Square Association was incorporated in 1967 to encourage restoration of Union Square and to work toward improved living conditions in the surrounding area.

Only 15 blocks west of the revitalized harbor, it was named a city historic and architectural preservation district in 1967. The boundaries were enlarged in 1978 and extend from Schroeder St. to Fulton Ave. (E-W) and from W. Baltimore St. to W. Pratt and W. Lombard Sts. (N-S). In 1983 it was listed on the National Register of Historic Places.

HISTORY IN PROCESS . . . . .

1799 - Willowbrook, the country estate of Thorowgood Smith, the second mayor, was built immediately west of Union Square.

1820's - Development began along nearby Baltimore St., a major thoroughfare connecting Baltimore with the West.

1837 - Hollins Market was established. The present restored market is the oldest in continuous use in the city.

1847 - Union Square was ceded to the city for perpetual use as a public park. Willowbrook was further divided, and construction of the first houses began. By 1890, housing in the area was complete with a diversity of Victorian styles reflecting the heterogeneity of the developing neighborhood.

1867 to 1965 - Willowbrook served as the House of the Good Shepard for deliquent girls.

1880's - The area became a center for German and later Lithuanian life and activity. The iron fence and ornate gates were removed from the park and replaced with large cast iron urns.

1883 to 1956 - H.L. Mencken, the "Bard of Baltimore" and friend of a number of

current residents lived at 1524 Hollins St.

1940's to 1960's - The iron urns and the Square's fountain were smelted down for use in the war effort. Many houses were divided into apartments to meet the increasing urban demands.

By the late 60's, a number of the Baltimore St. businesses declined.

In 1965, Willowbrook was razed to allow construction of the Steuart Hill Elementary School. The mansion's Oval Room has been preserved in the Baltimore Museum of Art.

1965 to 1976 - Private restoration of area homes was started in an effort to halt further destruction. This effort lead to the formation of the Union Square Association in 1967, the historic preservation designation in 1970, and the beginning of the restoration of Union Square Park.

1977 - The nation's first shopsteading program was inaugurated to encourage revitalization of the W. Baltimore St. commercial district.

1983 - H.L. Mencken home was acquired by the city and opened as the Mencken Museum. The Union Square/Hollins Market area is listed in the National Register.

———————

As an historical and architectural preservation district, the exteriors of the homes are being preserved and restored along historical guidelines. However, the interiors are personal statements reflecting the diversity of interests and life styles of the residents.

———————

Paul Gilbert, Commercial Revitalization Coordinator
Department of Housing & Community Development
222 E. Saratoga Street - 5SMB

Urban Shopsteading

Commercial Revitalization   10/10/75
    Coordinating Committee

Late in May of this year, Herman Katkow and I attended a meeting of the West
Baltimore Street Merchants (Poppleton), at which plans for the Hollins Market
off-street parking lot and general commercial district rehabilitation were
discussed. At this same meeting, Mr. Katkow and I were introduced to
                         of the Union Square Association. In a discussion later that
evening,   was expressing her concern over vacant City-owned structures
located on West Baltimore Street, and outside of the existing Poppleton Urban
Renewal Area; and proposed a solution conceived as "urban shopsteading".

Conceptually, "shopsteading" would parallel the existing homesteading program
operated by DHCD. The only major difference proposed by   at that
time was a purchase price of $100 per vacant, city-owned, commercial structure.
She indicated that she was already aware of some interest in these properties
on the parts of a few potential "shopsteaders". Mr. Katkow and I were favorably
impressed by the concept and encouraged   to continue her efforts to
document interest in the subject properties.

Since our introduction, I have been in contact with   several times
concerning the development of the concept of "shopsteading". At our most recent
meeting, which included Ron Meckler of the Department of Planning, we developed
a proposed set of guidelines through which a "shopsteading" program could be
administered. That proposal is attached to this memo. Additionally,
presented a list of currently vacant, City-owned commercial structures; a list
of possible tax sale properties; and an expanded list of potential "shopsteaders".
With the assistance of both Meckler and myself,   will graphically
represent the properties in question at the Coordinating Committee meeting of
October 10.

The mechanics of such a program, as presented in the attachment, seem rather
straightforward; however, resolution of the proposed guidelines must be achieved
by the Coordinating Committee in order to avoid conflict with the broad policy
and goals of the Commercial District Improvement Program. Specific points for
resolution include the "shopsteading" of nonconforming land uses, impact on
existing small businesses, "shopsteading" business failures, plans and design
standards for areas of extensive "shopsteading", etc. Resolution of the above
items and other anticipated "problems and exceptions" would permit the City-wide

applicability of such a program.

Adequate financing of a "shopsteading" program is critical. Incentive to homestead is provided by the property purchase price of $1, and also the availability of REAL money with which to rehabilitate. The purchase price of $100 for a commercial structure is alluring to a prospective "shopsteader", yet due to the prior commitments of the Commercial REAL to the six priority districts, severe limitations on that bond money would seem to preclude its use for financing an extensive "shopsteading" program. An alternative means of funding such a program seems to exist in the form of the SBA 502 program.   has been in touch with Mr. Michael McNiel of the Baltimore SBA office, and is aware of the SBA 502 program. Additionally, she has assembled the necessary twenty-five persons to form the required (West Baltimore Street) LDC.   will continue working with Mr. McNiel in order to establish a working partnership in administering the 502 program in the above area.

     will make an appearance at the Coordinating Committee meeting of October 10th in order to 1) present her concept of "shopsteading"; 2) outline criteria of the program in general; 3) discuss the immediate implementation potential of 1300-1600 West Baltimore Street, in particular; and 4) to request City financial participation in the LDC to a maximum of $50,000, in order to leverage potentially $450,000 from SBA, assuming 502 money availability.

In the final analysis, it is my opinion that the concept is both imaginative and practical, and should be endorsed "in principle" by the Committee. The use of the Commercial REAL money can generate larger amounts of concentrated reinvestment in the West Baltimore Street area in a relatively short period of time, and could produce high visibility improvements as a result of the Self-Help Program. Assuming the Committee's endorsement of the concept, I would like to continue working with   in finalizing the details of the program and initiating its implementation on West Baltimore Street.

PGilbert:cp

Compl.cc: Mr. Berkowitz
           Mr. Katkow
           Mr. Oppel
           Mr. Raich

cc: Mr. Embry
     Mr. Brodie
     Mr. Gilbert
     Planning

Special Criteria for Urban Shopsteading

*Note: If not specifically indicated in this list, existing guidelines for urban homesteading would apply to the concept of "Shopsteading."

Acquisition and Sequence Recommendations

- Structure must be vacant and City-owned.

- Structure must be located in a commercial zoning district; proposed commercial use must be a permitted use in the particular zoning district; "shopsteading" of a non-conforming land use, i.e. Ma & Pa corner store, shall conform to all existing review processes and be reviewed by Commission of DHCD.

- Acquisition price for structure and property shall be $100.

- The proposed business shall be established within six (6) months.

- Code requirements shall be met within one (1) year.

- "Shopsteader must occupy or manage (as a branch location) the business which is established for a period of two (2) years, assuming business viability.

- Business failure can result in the resale of the structure and property within the initial two year period, subject to approval of new buyer by the Commissioner of DHCD.

- At end of two (2) year period, the structure and property belong to the individual "shopsteader."

- "Shopsteaders" may purchase more than one property based on business needs and with approval of Commissioner of DHCD.

Renovation Recommendations

- The property shall be rehabilitated to meet City Building Code requirements; if the property is located within an urban renewal or historic area, it shall be rehabilitated to meet standards which are higher and/or stricter if those standards are enacted; rehabilitation standards resulting from State or Federal programs shall be enforced.

- Plans for rehabilitation shall be reviewed by the Commissioner of DHCD, the DAP (optional), and all appropriate reviewing agencies.

Inspections

- Inspection of property shall occur in a similar manner to that in the homesteading program, i.e. prior to transaction, periodically, and at the end of the rehabilitation period.

- Additionally, inspections should occur in commercial area adjacent to "shopstead" property in order to complement and reinforce the program.

Financing

- SBA 502

- Availability of Residential REAL for rehabilitation of upper floor apartments in a later phase.

- Implementation of Commercial District Improvement Plan (later phase) and CIP items to establish quid pro quo.

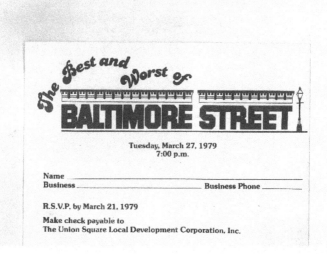

The Best and Worst of

BALTIMORE STREET

Tuesday, March 27, 1979
7:00 p.m.

Name _____

Business _____ Business Phone _____

R.S.V.P. by March 21, 1979

Make check payable to
The Union Square Local Development Corporation, Inc.

There were so many phenomenal employees working for the City of Baltimore who got hung up in the web of corruption. I know of several who were blackmailed into silence because of sexual preferences and addictions. I will never forget the day I answered the ring at my back door and greeted a well-respected DHCD employee wearing a top coat who asked for my assistance. The individual stated he was gay but did not want to get entrapped in a recent investigation of pedophiles. I listened in disbelief as he described a work environment where men were routinely subjected to sexual harassment. He had been subjected to verbal abuse with the comment, "Oh goody, more panties to get into," on his second day behind a desk at DHCD. I, too, had been subjected to ostracism for daring to demand an end to sexual child molestation, a.k.a. pedo-philia. Some Union Square residents refused to believe pe-dophiles in the community were molesting children—mostly males—and their denials had horrifying conse-quences. Had two community leaders been vigorously prosecuted for their first documented offenses, there most likely would not have been the sixty-four counts of child molestation the employee came to see me concerning. There was a detailed diary kept by those arrested, which was sequestered by the state attorney office. There was no trial. The defendants took an Alford plea and none of the injured minors received counseling. There was a complete cover-up.

I had been photographed by photographer Roger Miller for *Baltimore Magazine*—quite an honor—as one of the eight most powerful women in Maryland. Because I refused to back off the pedophile abuse in Union Square and Baltimore, I was deleted from the article. A small price to pay for defending the honor of children and a commu-nity. One DHCD antagonist actually wrote a letter to the *Baltimore Sun* vilifying me. That, too, was an honor. Kurt Schmoke became mayor, William Donald Schaefer be-came governor, and pedophiles remained protected. My second book, *Broken Zipper*, details how some legislators' and community leaders' votes were controlled by black-mail. Someone needs to locate the sequestered diary and open a full investigation into why no action was taken by some legislators on issues involving these criminal acts.

Several months ago, I drove through the Union Square Historic District just to see how things were going. I was dismayed to see so many dilapidated houses—peeling paint, broken windows, boarded openings on homes which had once been restored. Fortunately, there were the well-maintained homes of longtime residents which were in excellent condition and reflected the community in a more positive way. It is difficult to understand why the historic district is not in pristine condition. Obviously, code enforcement is lacking. Also lacking is any annual inspection by local, state, and federal preservation organizations. These people jokingly used to be called "martini-sipping preservationists" who cared very little about the west side of Baltimore. As luck would have it, there were true preservationists who were ardent advocates of West Baltimore history, which include the H. L. Mencken and Edgar Allan Poe homes. I actually met a newer resident from the 1400 block of Hollins Street who lamented the condition of West Baltimore Street. He stated there was nothing the Union Square Association could do because the north side of the street was in a different urban renewal area. I corrected him on this bit of information and had to explain where I got my facts. I tried to keep it low-key but had to point out that he had been grossly misinformed and challenged him to educate not only himself but the community.

Romaine Somerville, the director of the Commission for Historical and Architectural Preservation (CHAP), was an amazing leader. She worked diligently to guide us through the process of becoming a local and national historic district.

There had been a huge fire in one of the multi-family rental units on the Square shortly before paperwork was submitted. Mrs. Somerville had advised us that we had little chance of getting the designated status if "a tooth" was missing from the square. Christmas morning, I was in awe when I opened an envelope containing my Christmas gift from my mother and father-in-law—the deed to the burned structure at 1528 Hollins Street which had been slated for demolition.

The night of the inferno, I met a superb reporter from the *Baltimore Sun* papers, Earl Arnett. It was Earl who introduced me to Aubrey Bodine, famed Baltimore photographer who would later photograph us for the cover of the *Sun Magazine*. They stopped by our home at 1504 Hollins Street some weeks later, and trying to be courteous, I offered something cold to drink. At the time, I did not know Bodine was a diabetic who sometimes cheated! He complimented me on the sweetened Lipton iced tea and shortly after they left, Bodine was in the emergency room. I called the *Sun* papers to apologize to Bodine, who laughed and apologized for not telling me he was a diabetic. Said he was sending me a small gift to make it better. When the manila envelope arrived, I could not believe the contents: auto-graphed Bodine photographs of the H. L. Mencken House at 1524 Hollins Street and autographed negatives of Union Square. Earl Arnett also introduced me to Baltimore's First Lady of Jazz, Ethel Ennis, the night he invited us to Ethel's place in Mount Vernon. It turned out Ethel Ennis was his wife. What an amazing couple.

MEMORANDUM

WILLIAM DONALD SCHAEFER
President
Baltimore City Council
307 City Hall
Baltimore, Maryland 21202

TO: Dr. F. Pierce Linaweaver

FROM: William Donald Schaefer

DATE: April 16, 1969

RE: Union Square Area — Hollins Street

The residents in the Union Square area (1500 block Hollins Street) are in the process of "upgrading the area". There have been substantial improvements of the property made surrounding the Square including the H. L. Mencken house at 1524 Hollins Street.

A future project of the residents is the restoration of Union Square as originally built. Investigation seems to indicate that the sidewalks were pink and white. After the initial shock wears off, this may not be completely farfetched.

The purpose of this memorandum is to determine whether there are any plans to repave Union Square in the near future.

I would appreciate your looking into this matter and advising me of your findings.

WILLIAM DONALD SCHAEFER

cc: Mr. Douglas S. Tawney

CITY OF BALTIMORE

WILLIAM DONALD SCHAEFER, Mayor

DEPARTMENT OF HOUSING AND
COMMUNITY DEVELOPMENT

ROBERT C. EMBRY, JR., Commissioner
222 East Saratoga Street, Baltimore, Maryland 21202

NOV 4 1975

1532 Hollins Street
Baltimore, Maryland 21223

Subject: 1524 Hollins Street
(H. L. Mencken Home)

Thank you for bringing to my attention the matter concerning the H. L. Mencken
Home. As you know, the property is now owned by the University of Maryland.

Our records show that the property is to be used for two dwelling units and one
office. However, an inspection on September 25, 1975 revealed that the office
had been converted into an apartment without any record of a permit application
being filed. This Department has contacted the president of the University of
Maryland and apprised him of this fact and put the University on notice that they
would either have to vacate the apartment or apply for a change in the permitted
use of this property.

I understand that both George H. Ball, Chief of Field Operations for the West
Area and James Dembeck, Zoning Administrator, have discussed this case with you
and that Mr. Ball has informed you that if and when an appeal to the Board of
Municipal and Zoning Appeals is made by the University of Maryland to use the
premises for three dwelling units you will be notified. I can assure you that
this Department will diligently pursue this matter until it has been satisfacto-
rily resolved.

Again, thank you for bringing this matter to my attention and for your continued
interest in the Union Square Area. The persons on my staff most familiar with this
matter are George H. Ball, who can be reached at 1313 Druid Hill Avenue, telephone
number 396-0075 and James Dembeck, who can be reached at 222 E. Saratoga Street,
telephone number 396-4185.

Sincerely yours,

R. C. EMBRY, JR.
Commissioner

December 18, 1973

Dr. Albin O. Kuhn
Chancellor
University of Maryland
Greene and Redwood Streets
Baltimore, Maryland 21201

Dear Dr. Kuhn:

During our meeting regarding the residence of H. L. Mencken you recommended that the Union Square Association develop a proposal for utilizing the Mencken residence which could be presented at the next meeting with the Deans of the various departments within the University.

The Union Square Association would like to restore the first floor and garden of 1524 Hollins Street and establish visiting hours. The residence would be staffed by volunteers with some knowledge of the community and Mencken. Donations and proceeds from lectures and the sale of written material would fund the proposal.

Various historical groups have expressed interest in this project such as aiding in recovering furniture and developing historical displays. The Commission for Historical and Architectural Preservation has expressed great interest because this property is within the boundaries of the Union Square Historical and Architectural Preservation District. There is no example of a restored parlor and library from that period according to Miss Deborah Ann Claiborne, Executive Secretary for the Commission. Beautiful Baltimore, Inc., and the Maryland House and Garden Tour sponsors have offered to assist with landscape restoration.

I want to thank you for your interest and for presenting these recommendations to the Deans. Please contact me at 566-0644 if additional information is needed.

Sincerely,

1114 Bellemore Road
Baltimore, Md. 21210
March 10, 1977

Hon. William Donald Schaefer, Mayor
City Hall
Baltimore, Md. 21202

Dear Mayor Schaefer,

    The Baltimore City Committee of the Maryland Historical Trust
has been aware for some time of the City's efforts and progress in
the preservation of Union Square. Now, we understand that there is
a possibility of acquiring the Henry Mencken House at 1524 Hollins
Street and opening part of it to the many visitors who have so far
been frustrated in their attempts to see inside the home of the
"Sage of Baltimore". I am writing to tell you that this committee
fully supports you in your attempts to acquire the house and that
we believe it would be another in the many noteworthy achievements
of your administrations.

                Sincerely,

                Mrs. Walter E. Black, Jr.
                Chairman

CHAPTER NINE

Ransomware attacks have become common with urban areas scrambling to recover missing data. Is it possible that a compromised area used an alleged ransomware attack to destroy computerized data documenting monetary abuses and fraudulent activity? Driving through Baltimore today, one can see hundreds of clear parcels—almost a "Greening of Baltimore movement"—awaiting development. The State of Maryland provided supplemental funds to Baltimore, ostensibly to improve blighted areas by demolishing deteriorated structures. The reality was that physical evidence of massive fraud involving public monies was being destroyed. Coupled with a cyberattack, one would think a cover-up might work. Wrong! A comparison of addresses to federal block grant applications and granting performance reports readily documents this massive scam which has gone on for decades.

Donald Trump noted large sums of money which have gone to blighted urban areas and acknowledged there is no accountability for the funds. Urban areas need to explain how all of this federal funding was used, since it obviously was not spent for the stated purposes. Legislators need to be held accountable for areas which have remained blighted for decades. Race and gender become an issue when federal funding was exclusively available based on skin color or sex. The infamous no-bid contracts were doomed from conception with little, if any, oversight.

In some instances, contractors went from state to state, defaulting on every project. In the case of Baltimore, it was never determined who was responsible for inviting Mecca Construction to participate in the program when the company had defaulted in other states.

The concept of Washington being a swamp is an easy sell. What is not being stated clearly is that no sane person would want to be elected to this swamp full of corrupt flesh-eating bacteria if the candidate was aware of the corruption which has been tolerated for decades. Every election, neophyte candidates vie to become a part of this controlled chaos being operated like a malfunctioning organized crime syndicate run by Nancy Pelosi. Surely, over the decades, she was made aware of urban financial chaos by elected representatives and had the power to investigate.

The City of Baltimore hired some young professionals with expertise in writing block grant proposals, and this is when things began to go awry. For decades, the City of

Baltimore had stockpiled vacant properties, and this presented the perfect opportunity to obtain federal monies to acquire and rehab vacant or dilapidated structures. Of course, for years, HUD has been giving Baltimore funds to secure and stabilize the same structures. Public hearings had to be held and well-intended residents showed up to buy into plans being submitted. Residents assumed all documents being forwarded to government agencies were legitimate. Concepts were approved often without specific addresses.

I owe a lot to Charles Blount, a.k.a. "Nigger Charlie," who owned and operated the Hee Haw Lounge located in the 900 block of West Baltimore Street. I met Mr. Blount during a blizzard in Baltimore when I was trying to thumb a ride at West Baltimore and Gilmore streets. My baby was very ill and I had to get to an emergency room, but absolutely no transportation was available. An expensive car pulled up to the corner where I was standing. When the window rolled down, a man wearing a fur-trimmed coat and fur hat asked what I was doing out in the snow with my baby. He knew my name, and when I explained how desperate I was to get to the University of Maryland emergency room, he told his driver to help me into the car. Not only did he take me to the emergency room, but they also came back to get me later. In route, Mr. Blount indicated he had been told to contact me by Sterling

Stanfield, whose property had been fraudulently included in a funding proposal, about problems he was having with the Department of Housing and Community Development. He gave me his address and phone numbers that night and told me to ask for "Nigger Charlie" when I came in—that is, if I wanted to see him, because that is what his friends and people who were okay called him. He said the city was trying to force him out of business and that he was told they needed his property for urban renewal purposes.

I had never seen a grantee performance report until Charles Blount piqued my interest. When I tried to get a copy of the one covering that area, the information was not readily available. I was told the Enoch Pratt Free Library was the designated repository for public access to these documents. The copy was not on the shelves at the Pratt Library, so a replacement was ordered. When I went back to the Pratt to get the report, it, too, was missing. A third copy was ordered and the Pratt employee kept it in an undisclosed location until I could get there to pick it up. When I got the document, it was like putting the last puzzle piece in place on a thousand-piece puzzle. The grantee performance report was a joke—it was obvious HUD employees were not going to the physical locations checking the status of projects prior to releasing funds or signing off on funds already received by the Department of Housing and Community Development.

My visit to the Hee Haw Lounge was an awakening. The first floor had the traditional built-in bar with vintage bar stools. The walls were decorated with boxing posters and gallon jars of pickled pigs' feet, pickled onions, and miscellaneous snacks were on the bar. I could never have dreamed what was on the upper floors, which was not open to every walk-in patron. I asked for "Nigger Charlie" as instructed and was taken up a small flight of stairs to a chic club right out of New Orleans. The decor was amazing, as was the liquor selection. There simply was no reason to put this entrepreneur out of business and condemn his property. As we talked, I was forthright about my concerns and left feeling like I had a trusted ally in trying to deal with the Department of Housing and Community Development.

A meeting was arranged with the local HUD office in Baltimore by investigators. Outside individuals were not to be aware of the meeting and my identity was to be protected. The meeting mood was tense as I presented the contents of my infamous Red Envelope, which documented example after example of fraud. At one point, the individual we were meeting with asked facetiously what I expected HUD to do about this. My unprofessional response was, "Tell your employees to get up off their lazy asses" and go look at these sites. I emphatically stated

Housing and Urban Development was partially responsible and needed to start an investigation. When the meeting ended, the environment was one of hostility. As I stood in the hallway outside, I heard glass break and the exclamation, "That b****, who does she think she is?" Within minutes, I received a call from a sympathizer within the Department of Housing and Community Development telling me the commissioner's office had been told of the meeting by Housing and Urban Development. The battle was clearly on!

For almost a year, I had been trying to get a list of properties available for sale from the DHCD, to no avail. Some individuals posing as developers went down to the Land Disposition Office and left with a single sheet of paper listing fewer than twenty properties. It was only by visiting the back office that a larger list was available. Then, there was the carefully guarded list created as a result of shuffling money and false grantee performance reports.

For almost a year, I had also been trying to obtain a list of buildings owned or controlled by the Housing Authority of Baltimore City (HABC) and quasi-public entities. After the debacle at the HUD meeting, I received a phone call from a DHCD employee advising me that she had been asked what paperwork I was trying to get and was told to notify supervisors whenever I came in. To this date, I do not know the identity of the Department of Housing and Community Development employee who called and told me to come down ASAP to pick up what I needed. It was emphasized the originals had to be back in two hours. I called a copy shop on East Baltimore Street to ensure expedited handling and grabbed a cab. I had been told to bring a large coat to throw over the printout to ensure confidentiality. I went to the designated doorway and an arm suddenly thrust the printout to me. Under the coat it went and I kept walking. The cost of printing came to over two hundred dollars, which was paid in cash—no one wanted this transaction to be traced. I walked back to the Department of Housing and Community Development, walked to the same doorway, and placed the documents on a table as instructed. The investigative agencies I was working with made copies.

The next day I started cross-referencing block grant applications, grantee performance reports, and photographs. I was truly horrified to document irregularity after irregularity and became more positive each day that massive fraud had taken place routinely. Meetings were quietly set up at night with trusted community leaders to get an explanation. It was obvious that trust had been misplaced, but no one wanted to confront individual leaders at the Department of Housing and Community Development for fear of losing future funding requests.

I agreed to attend public hearings on funding and raise objections when properties or funding were on the agenda impacting our area. Local residents would show up to indicate an interest and demonstrate off-the-record support.

After Kurt Schmoke became mayor, the situation became far worse. Schaefer had stayed on top of things in West Baltimore, and we benefited from his "do it now" policies.

We had to come up with a strategy to try to force the City of Baltimore to come into compliance with its own laws. One proposal was to get a judge to issue a writ of mandamus ordering the city to develop, within six months, a plan to dispose of all vacant properties within one year. Not only would this proposal place properties back in the hands of private citizens, it would end the backroom corruption of deciding who had access to real estate on a preferential basis. Transparency was what we were seeking as well as equality.

Then, there was the equitable enforcement of CHAP guidelines. We sought to have a judge order the agency to come into compliance by abiding by its imperative duty to enforce the CHAP ordinance. We knew there had been at least one prior case involving "demolition by neglect" but could not get the state attorney to turn over records of that case.

As a last resort, we threatened to ask that all federal funding to Baltimore be denied until the issues of corruption were resolved. It was no secret that Baltimore City was in big trouble. The *Baltimore Sun* had a superb investigative reporter document massive fraud in the no-bid housing contracts. Councilwoman Vera Hall insisted the city council not open an investigation, stating her sham of a hearing had already reviewed these issues. She knew documents substantiating fraud had been blocked from introduction at the public hearing she conducted. What elected officials did not know was that this incriminating evidence was in the hands of the FBI and an investigation was underway.

James Cabezas had indicated each signature on a false document would support, at the least, a charge of perjury. He emphasized that his office did not have jurisdiction but wanted to be kept informed. I am grateful to him for the encouragement and expertise he offered.

I had heard rumors about an inquiry into land transactions around Camden Yards—the new baseball stadium—and was requested to attend a meeting with the head of the Nexus unit at 301 West Preston Street. It was my understanding that some individuals with political connections were receiving lucrative relocation money because of insider information. It was reported that some businesses merely changed names and addresses to the

COMMITTEES:
Banking, Finance & Urban Affairs
Small Business
Joint Economic Committee

SUB-COMMITTERS:
Minority Enterprise, Finance and
Urban Development, Chairman
Procurement, Taxation and Tourism
Housing & Community Development
Financial Institutions Supervision

MEMBER:
Congressional Black Caucus, Chairman
Caucus of Women's Issues
Congressional Arts Caucus
Federal Government
Service Task Force

WASHINGTON OFFICE:
2419 Rayburn Building
Washington, D.C. 20515
202/225-4741

DISTRICT OFFICES:
3000 Druid Park Drive
Baltimore, MD 21215
410/367-1900

1825 Woodlawn Drive
Suite 106
Baltimore, MD 21207
410/298-5997

2203 N. Charles Street
Baltimore, MD 21218
410/235-2700

Congress of the United States
House of Representatives
Washington, D.C. 20515

KWEISI MFUME
7TH DISTRICT, MARYLAND

September 12, 1994

Ms. Ardebella Fox
1424 Hollins Street
Baltimore, Maryland 21223

Dear Ms. Fox:

This communication comes to acknowledge receipt of your correspondence regarding the deteriorating vacant properties in the Union Square/Hollins Market area.

I appreciate your concern and will help any way I can. I have contacted Daniel Henson, Executive Director, Baltimore City Housing Authority, on your behalf and will be back in touch with you once I receive a response from him.

In the meantime, please feel free to contact my staff assistant, Jennine Auerbach at 367-1900 if you have any questions.

Sincerely,

Kweisi Mfume
Member of Congress

KM/sf

SEP – 6 1994

Ms. Ardebella Dean Fox
1424 Hollins Street
Baltimore, MD   21223

Dear Ms. Fox:

Thank you for your letter dated July 15, 1994, to
Secretary Henry Cisneros requesting assistance in correcting what
you perceive as an inequitable distribution of funds and the
neglect of Southwest Baltimore by the City of Baltimore. You
express particular concern for the Union Square-Hollins Market
area which is both a local and national historic district. Since
my office is responsible for the administration of the Community
Development Block Grant (CDBG) program, your letter has been
referred to my office for response.

Housing rehabilitation, demolition, and interim assistance
for trash removal are eligible activities under the CDBG program.
This program, authorized under Title I of the Housing and
Community Development Act of 1974, as amended, provides annual
grants on a formula basis to entitled cities and counties to
implement a wide variety of community and economic development
activities which are initiated and developed at the local level
based upon a community's perception of its local needs,
priorities, and benefit to the community. The Department of
Housing and Urban Development (HUD) requires that the activity
meet certain requirements, including that it be eligible and meet
one of the following broad national objectives: benefit persons
of low and moderate income, aid in the prevention or elimination
of slums or blight, or meet other community development needs of
a particular urgency. The City of Baltimore received a CDBG
allocation of $30,711,000 in Fiscal Year 1994.

Prior to receiving its annual grant, each recipient must
prepare a proposed statement of community development objectives
and projected use of funds describing the activities that the
grantee proposes to carry out with anticipated CDBG funds. This
statement must be in sufficient detail, including location, to
allow citizens to determine the degree to which they will be

affected and must be furnished to citizens in a manner which provides for timely examination, appraisal, and comment. The grantee must follow a citizen participation plan which describes the jurisdiction's plan for affording affected citizens an opportunity to provide comments on the proposed statement. You may wish to ask the City for a copy of its citizen participation plan in order to more fully participate in this process.

In addition to the above requirements, the grantee must submit to the Department an annual report (Grantee Performance Report) which describes the grantee's accomplishments over the past year. Copies of this report should be made available to citizens in sufficient time to permit citizens an opportunity to comment on the report prior to its submission to HUD. A summary of citizens' comments is submitted to HUD along with the annual performance report.

The City has considerable discretion in determining where and how its CDBG funds are expended. The Department does not have the authority to intervene in this process unless there is some aspect of the grantee's program that violates Federal regulations. Based on information provided by the Department's Baltimore Office, virtually all of the City's housing is historic. Because the City's community development needs outweigh the available funding, the City has identified target areas where a concentrated amount of CDBG funds is expended. Both CDBG and Urban Development Action Grant funds have been used to address the deterioration of the housing stock.

Since CDBG funds are not provided directly to individuals or other entities by the Federal Government, I recommend that you continue to work with City officials to make the community development needs of your neighborhood known. The local contact person is Mr. Daniel P. Henson, III, Commissioner, Department of Housing and Community Development, 417 East Fayette Street, Baltimore, Maryland 21202. Mr. Henson's telephone number is (410) 396-3422.

Enclosed is a Fact Sheet which provides additional information on the CDBG program. Thank you for your interest in the Department's programs.

Very sincerely yours,

James R. Broughman
Director, Office of Block
Grant Assistance

1424 Hallens Street
Baltimore, Maryland 21223
July 15, 1994

The Honorable Kurt L. Schmoke
Mayor
City of Baltimore
City Hall
100 North Holiday Street
Baltimore, Maryland 21202

Ref: Housing

Dear Mayor Schmoke:

As you are aware The Union Square-Hallens Market area is both a local and National Historic District. It is inconceivable that properties are being allowed to deteriorate when enforcement of The Housing Code and "Demolition by Neglect" provision of the Commission for Historical and Architectural Preservation ordinance exist. Ours is a preservation oriented community which should present stability rather than on going decay.

Attempts to resolve issues in the courts and field offices with Housing and

Community Development have failed. It would be most unfortunate if to preserve the integrity of our community we would have to take action to block the flow of funds to Baltimore City.

We are requesting immediate action on the following properties. We have enclosed pictures.

100 South Stricker St
100 South Mount St.
1700 West Lombard St.
1703, 1707, 1717 West Lombard St.
    54, 43 South Fulton
1727, 1721, 1717, 1715, 1711, 1708, 1707 Hollins St.
1716, 1714, 1712, 1718, 1720 Frederick Ave.
114, 112 South Mount St.
17 South Calhoun
200, 201, 203, 209, 211, 204, 232 South Gilmore
125, 134 South Gilmore
1121 Hollins
1008 West Lombard
1225, 1242 West Lombard - 1311, 1322, 1414 W. Lomba

Copy: Honorable Mary Pat Clarke   Sincerely,
      Senator Barbara Mikulski
      Senator Paul Sarbanes   Ardabella Fox
      Honorable Henry Cisneros

new property being traded for redevelopment. The meeting was challenging as I was asked what I had learned about property disposition by the Department of Housing and Community Development—what did it take to gain access to the total list of properties available? A follow-up meeting was scheduled for two weeks later. When I arrived for that meeting, I immediately knew something was wrong. The office was empty. I was told the person I met with had died suddenly and all paperwork had been picked up by individuals in Annapolis. No one knew the answers to basic questions. Who picked up the documents, where were they taken, and what individual would be picking up on this inquiry? I was pleased I had not given up too much information at the initial meeting.

When everything was going right for the Union Square West Baltimore Street area, tragedy struck. We were working with Carl Ruskin, one of the best planners ever, when he was killed while attending an herb festival in Leakin Park in a freak accident. A bolt of lightning struck the church where he and others had taken shelter during the storm. Carl Ruskin had grasped the vision of what the community needed and wanted—the ability to make dreams become reality by implementing designs and timetables. He recognized the uniqueness of our urban area and did not roll over in the face of adversity. We were lauded for our creativity and progressive ideas, but there were those who felt West Baltimore should be the last frontier for development. I was totally repulsed but could say nothing publicly when the Shopsteading program premier featured a block in East Baltimore because West Baltimore was "too dark." This was absolute racism, but the show went on.

Shopsteading on West Baltimore Street was truly unique, as were the amazing "shopsteaders." Media coverage was ample but it was a constant battle for survival. Located just east of the infamous hole where *The Wire* was filmed, drugs were always an issue. The Baltimore City Police Department stepped up and overlapping patrols of Baltimore Street, which was the dividing line between the southern and western police districts, helped.

Every so often, a boarded entrance "fence" or graffiti-covered wall would have the dreaded RIP—all in caps—spray-painted for all to see. In an effort to make the street safer, I would try to get some background information on what led to the RIP signs. At one point, I was told it wasn't always a territorial dispute that involved local dealers. Some of the guys dealing said it was "crooked cops" taking people out to ensure they would not give information to legitimate officers. This was not the first time I had heard claims of illegal contact by rogue officers. Charles Blount had told me there were some cops who would plant evidence if a bust came up empty. One officer asked me to help expedite a transfer to the motorcycle division because he did not like the way some things were going down and felt unsafe. He stated impending raids were not being kept confidential.

There was an incident on South Carrollton Avenue when an elderly woman observed what she called the shakedown of a young dealer as he exited the Hollins Market liquor store. His pockets were bulging with money and she was certain the teenage dealer was robbed before the man she described as a Baltimore City police officer had taken everything out of his pockets, patted him on the shoulders, and let him run west on Lemon Street. She claimed she filed a complaint but got no response. I got a detailed description of this alleged officer from her and, after many phone calls, was able to determine that the person could not have been a legitimate officer but was an imposter. There were, however, two officers who were identified as corrupt, and this proved to be just reason for concern.

On November 3, 1984, one of Baltimore's finest officers, Marcellus Ward, lost his life when a drug raid was being conducted at 1829 Frederick Avenue. To this day, there are unanswered questions. It appeared the raid had been leaked by unidentified corrupt officers.

As a nation, we have finally acknowledged that opium

addiction is a major problem. For decades, this issue was ignored and functioning addicts could not allow their addictions to become known. Anyone with knowledge of their habit would be in a position of control, which made that person very vulnerable. It was for this reason that some bills we tried to get introduced were never scheduled for hearings. There was one very powerful functioning addict actually working in the city solicitor's office and, obviously, under control of the wrong individuals. But we still tried to bring about change, and I did not expose this person. He had a career, wife, children, and a "monkey on his back." We actually became friends when I heard of his plight.

CHAPTER TEN

Were it not for the Baltimore City paper, there would have been little coverage of the debacle at the City Hall housing hearing on March 7, 1995. "The Top 10 of 1995 Days in the News" by Van Smith and Deirdre Shesgreen summarizes the housing hearing conducted by City Council Vice President Vera Hall as being engineered to "prevent probing questions from council members and the public" regarding the $25.6 million no-bid public housing repair program. Lawrence Bell III, who called the hearing a "charade," later ran for city council president and won. It was stated the manner in which Vera Hall handled the hearing became an election issue when she ran against Bell and lost.

City Council President Mary Pat Clarke showed leadership when she revived the Legislative Investigations Committee the week after the Hall hearing. I had met with Mrs. Clarke on several occasions to seek her assistance in dealing with corruption in the Department of Housing and Community Development. She had also been present at the

Board of Estimates hearings when the agency's actions were challenged.

There is little doubt my civil rights were violated at the March 7 hearing, and in my opinion, federal charges should have been brought against every individual who was involved. The spectators in the balcony were shouting to Mrs. Hall to let me testify. She ordered them to leave the council chambers. A uniformed officer from Mayor Schmoke's office, according to John Elsberry, who was exiting the balcony, demanded to know what I was still doing in the council chambers and why I had not been "forcibly removed." I will always be grateful to the non-racist members of the city council who acted to protect me. I was absolutely stunned at what transpired at the hearing. I should have known something was up when Arnold Jolivet called me twice that day suggesting I not attend and assured me all concerns would be addressed.

Councilwoman Hall played a pivotal role in trying to shut down the investigation. The well-documented *Baltimore Sun*'s three-part investigative article, published in February, was called a lie. She expected everyone would agree with her. Protesters, at an organized rally in front of City Hall, carried signs supporting Mayor Schmoke and the corrupt housing administration.

The complex system put in place to defraud the federal

government can be likened to organized crime. It is inconceivable that such a scam has gone on for decades. Day after day, elected officials in Baltimore have driven by rows of decaying properties in this city and have done absolutely nothing to bring about change. No one had publicly asked questions or demanded answers. Why? Because to ask the questions and get the answers would be to indict themselves. The filing of false documents with DHCD constituted criminal acts, according to James Cabezas, so why didn't anyone step up and report these incidents? When I came forward on March 7, 1995, and requested the investigation into Baltimore, a solution was also proposed. I wanted Baltimore to become a prototype for the nation by acknowledging past funding abuses coupled with a request for amnesty. Perhaps it was a bit of Pollyanna thinking, but I wanted Detroit, Trenton, Atlanta, Los Angeles, and any other major cities with financial solvency issues to be able to come forward and participate in a unique plan to create a new system of fiscal accountability. There would be no more blind-faith granting of funds and the release of monies unless it was digitally documented that the projects had been completed. I envisioned a new system where, with the "push of a button," everyone could see the phases of completion, funds requested, and funds released. There could be no more fraud.

Right now, many elected officials, primarily Democrats representing major American cities, are in a state of financial panic. These urban areas need money. In the past, applications for federal funds would have been submitted, many with false documentation to access funding. With a businessman, and builder, running America, it will be virtually impossible to get massive amounts of federal funds to renovate areas already allegedly renovated.

It is always easy to point out a problem; finding a solution designed to work can be very difficult. After much thought, I came up with the challenging but not unreasonable solution.

I wanted Baltimore City to become a prototype for the nation—and still do—after all these years. It has been stated correctly by President Trump that millions of dollars have been given to urban areas and he has asked what happened to the money. In my Pollyanna mind, Baltimore would draft a letter to President Trump stating that the City of Baltimore acknowledges numerous past funding abuses and requests amnesty from prosecution. The city would immediately implement a new system based on transparency and digital documentation. There could be no funding request submitted without digital images, and every municipality would be required to have trained individuals to perform these tasks. Once funding was approved, there could be no transfers of funds and no payouts to contractors until digital images were submitted. All projects could be reviewed online by individuals and elected officials with the push of a button.

The federal government would issue a mandate that all vacant, deteriorated properties be sold or slated for renovation within six months. There would be a virtual land rush creating jobs and an infusion of money into the economy.

As part of this new system, Baltimore and other participating cities in the amnesty program would be required to submit a financial solvency report, which would accurately show where existing deficits exist and make corrections. If an area opted not to participate in the amnesty program, a federal audit could begin with possible prosecution for fraud, since there is no statute of limitations.

It is surprising to see that Daniel P. Henson is in any way involved in development in Baltimore after the illegal fiasco he participated in—no, led—during the Schmoke administration. But, since the Clintons are no longer in the picture and Michael Braverman is in a position of powerful oversight, perhaps Henson can be useful—treat him like a well-educated, talented, remorseful convict on probation who was fortunate not to be in jail. Oops, did I say remorseful? But then, he appears to have just been one of Hillary's boys. Funny how in Baltimore many computer screens at DHCD were blank to prevent investigators from documenting outstanding abuses. It's like having a well-dressed, poised executive running an upscale dating service while being treated for several STDs—not a good thing!

There is little doubt that the federal government made massive amounts of money available to urban areas, like Baltimore, to fight blight. It was almost the worst form of behavior modification—rewarding an agency for failure rather than success. There were dollars to be had by maintaining a stockpile of vacant buildings, and with virtually no one doing a visual inspection, the same property could be used multiple times to obtain funding. Many segments of a report on the city's use of community-development block grants from March 1975 through December 1983, created when Marion W. Pines was housing commissioner, were pure fantasy.

The Union Square Community continues to battle HABC and DHCD over code enforcement and failure to keep vacant properties secure. This battle has continued for years, even decades. In 1991, a letter questions the need to ask that "an independent prosecutor be appointed to handle all cases involving M&CC Mayor and City Council owned structures."

City Council Bill 1230 was introduced in hopes of resolving the vacant building dilemma in our section of the city. By this time, equity in code enforcement had become a major issue, as had equal opportunity to purchase real estate for a personal residence or investment. The corrupt tentacles of DHCD, of which HABC was a part, had apparently not been recognized by the Schmoke administration, so growth was stymied in these areas. There was no logical systematic approach to inspections and enforcement. Some inspectors were perceived as being incompetent or corrupt when they were merely following orders not to do their jobs by DHCD when Daniel Henson was housing commissioner. As legislative liaison for the Union Square Association, I had gone "on loan" to COIL Inc., Communities Organized to Improve Life, an umbrella organization whose boundaries extended for more than the Union Square National Register District.

As president of the Union Square Local Development Corporation, I was able to carefully coordinate our plans for the commercial redevelopment of West Baltimore Street from Martin Luther King Jr. Boulevard West, incorporating the entirety of the Union Square National Register Area. From our perspective, it was rational to assume the University of Maryland might want to develop the 800–900 blocks of West Baltimore Street at some point. With this in mind, we refused to acquiesce on the rezoning of these blocks to residential and, with the support of COIL Inc., managed to win by defeating legislative attempts to rezone. It was truly amazing to see how many

Hollins Market merchants, West Baltimore Street businessmen, and residents from every income level would show up at the hearings. We showed multicolor-coded plans, which differentiated between owner-occupied and rental properties as prescribed by law in Baltimore. The theory before each hearing was to prepare to win a war, not a battle, and always watch the perimeter for the next battle. We were fighting for what we believed to be the soul of Baltimore City.

By the summer of 1994, Mayor Schmoke's office was being deluged with complaints regarding DHCD. At issue was the failure of the city to enforce the "Demolition By Neglect" provision of the CHAP ordinance. Letters to Secretary Henry Cisneros of HUD were responded to by the director of block grant assistance, James R. Browman, who referred the community back to Daniel Henson.

The letter to Mayor Schmoke stated, "Attempts to resolve issues in the courts and field offices with Housing and Community Development have failed. It would be most unfortunate if, to preserve the integrity of our community, we would have to take action to block the flow of funds to Baltimore City." If this sounded like a threat, it was. The intent was to have Housing and Community Development funds placed in escrow with the courts until Baltimore developed the plan to come into compliance with its own housing laws. Then, there was the falsification of grantee performance reports submitted to USDHCD, the United States Department of Housing and Community Development, which was clearly a criminal act designed to conceal theft or misappropriation of federal funds. Many legislators on the city, state, and federal level have been made aware of these documented criminal offenses but dared not stand up to the Democratic leadership of the city and demand corrective and punitive action.

It is unfortunate someone with the integrity and expertise of Nicole Faison was not on the scene during this period of time. It seems like everyone wanted to cut Mayor Kurt Schmoke a break. After all, he was the city's first black elected mayor and certainly had the qualifications on paper to lead Baltimore. In reality, Clarence Du Burns served as the city's first black mayor in 1987 when Schaefer became governor of the state of Maryland. Had someone like Miss Faison been available to Schmoke, she undoubtedly would have spotted the "game" of shuffling funds. In 1991, the City of Baltimore amended Block Grant 12 through 17 final statements, which involve the accounting for several million dollars. An analysis of block grant performance reports and on-site physical inspections would have called some of the reported activities into question.

It has been documented that the City of Baltimore has, for decades, endangered the public health, safety, and welfare of its citizens by maintaining pockets of blight— even fostering the development of additional blighted neighborhoods by failing to maintain areas once in pristine condition. From August 1990 until the infamous city council housing hearing sham, absolutely no elected officials challenged the city. In fairness, that does not imply that research was not underway to determine how the manipulation of federal funds developed and what could be done to take corrective action without damaging the reputation of the city. One legislator made me aware in the spring of 1995 that she had requested a list of all real estate owned or controlled by M&CC (mayor and city council), DHCD, or HABC, but received no response. I never told her that all of that information had been made available in a clandestine manner and was in the hands of an investigative agency.

The description of Washington politics being a swamp is fairly accurate but also simplistic. In the case of Baltimore and other major cities "playing the game," the swamp is infected with flesh-eating bacteria. Neophyte candidates from all over the US vie for political office with the intent of making a difference. Imagine what it must be like to realize that this so-called "swamp" can literally destroy you if you openly represent your constituents and do not back down. And what can realistically be expected of elected officials finding themselves in the middle of absolute corruption. One would think following the mandates for reporting such issues would bring results with a documented record of a complaint being reported, an investigation, and appropriate committee hearings.

Congressman Ben Cardin took the time to come and meet with me several times to go over documents, review photographs, and grasp the magnitude of these funding abuses. He was pensive and wanted to grasp both the timeline and extent of funding and real estate manipulation. When a major network in New York showed interest in interviewing me and filming footage, I was somewhat apprehensive but knew this corruption had to be exposed and the situation corrected. The interview and filming of street footage took place; the investigative agency had everything needed to get indictments and prosecute.

Congressman Ben Cardin, who could have, and should have, had the balls to demand an end to abuse of federal funds in Baltimore, appears to have done nothing tangible to correct the abuses. What did he do with the copies of documents he requested—why were they not turned over to a government oversight committee within Congress?

Please note that permits must be obtained from CHAP (396-4866) before any
exterior work is done on properties within the Union Square Historic District.

UNION SQUARE

Baltimore City Historic District Ordinance 821 6/2/70; 580 11/17/77
Certified Historic District for Tax Incentives 6/9/80
National Register of Historic Places 9/15/83
Description

The Union Square Historic District is a dense area of rowhouses and
commercial structures located approximately ten blocks west of the
Inner Harbor. Bounded by Schroeder, Pratt, Fulton, and Baltimore
Streets, the area is built on a grid street system which conforms to
the original 1818 layout of the area. The terrain gently slopes down
from west to east. There are two major features in the district.
Union Square Park, a speculative park and housing development of the
1840's, lies in the west; it is a block size park containing an
ornate fountain and a Greek Revival Pavilion. In the east end lies
Hollins Market, an Italianate style market house, now the oldest
one existing in its original style in the city. The remainder of
the district developed after 1830 mainly as housing for workers in
nearby industries. These structures consist of low scale, two and
three story brick vernacular dwellings while larger, high style
rowhouses surround the park. Commercial structures were built
around Hollins Market, along South Carrollton Street, and along West
Baltimore Street (opened in 1807 as the Baltimore - Frederick
Turnpike). After the residential construction ended in the 1880's,
the commercial, as well as institutional, development continued and
these later buildings exhibit the architectural styles of the
early 20th century.

Significance

The Union Square Historic District is significant for its architecture
and history, which reflect the development of Urban America. The
district is a community of well-preserved rowhouses used for both
residential and commercial purposes and, as a result, it is a fine
example of a nineteenth century neighborhood. The district also
includes many significant individual structures which depict the
evolution of American architecture through the early twentieth ce .tury.
The plan of the district, and its park, manifest the changing concepts
of urban planning. The history and appearance of the district reveal
the tremendous economic impact of early and mid 19th century
industrialization resulting in expansion and the creation of new
neighborhoods in Baltimore. Two simultaneous events -- the advent of
the Baltimore and Ohio Railroad Shop at Pratt and Poppleton Streets and
a dramatic increase in foreign immigration in the 1830's -- initiated
construction in the district. Continued building booms and industrialization near the railroad maintained the physical growth. During this
period the Hollins Market was built (1838-1864) and the Donnell
family developed the Union Square Park and the surrounding area as a
speculative real estate venture (1845-c.1880), one of the earliest of
several such park projects in the City. While residential construction
ended about 1880, commercial and institutional buildings were built along
Baltimore Street (opened in 1887 as the Baltimore-Frederick Turnpike) and
around the market until the first quarter of the twentieth century.

6

The Union Square Bulletin

A Newsletter By and For the Members
of the Union Square Association

AUGUST 1990

"Be true to your work, your word and your friends." - Thoreau

PRESIDENT'S MESSAGE

In good faith, representatives of the Union Square Association attended a meeting conducted by CHAP and attended by representatives from Mayor Schmoke's office, Sally Wingo representing the City Council, representatives of the Baltimore City Planning Dept., Mr. Perry, a deputy commissioner from DHCD, Mr. John Huppert, Superintendent of Housing Inspection for the City of Baltimore, and Ron Miles, Program Manager for the Urban Renewal area. After listening to details of how the DHCD has failed to enforce code violations on properties owned or "controlled" by the Mayor and City Council/DHCD or quasi-public entities, I became enraged. Enraged because it was absolutely clear that DHCD feels it has the divine right to violate all preservation principles established in this community. Union Square residents are urged to walk by the properties within the boundaries of our community and place telephone calls to every level of government demanding immediate action of deteriorating structures. Mr. Huppert not only decides what goes to court, he also chairs the stabilization committee and therefore has the role of determining what is allowed to sit and deteriorate. He refuses to take the City to court. As citizens we need to ask whether it is necessary to have independent prosecutors handle these cases involving the City. We further need to demand that the addresses of the approximately 500 properties owned by the Mayor and City Council be printed in the Baltimore Sun and the Daily Record in addition to the stockpile of vacant properties "controlled" due to the "banking" of tax sale certificates.

Many of you attended the meeting at St. Martin's regarding the proposed demolition of 1608-1618 W. Baltimore St. The City refused to enforce the housing code even though capital improvements in the form of brick sidewalks and period lighting had been made. This lack of code enforcement was due to the fact that the Mayor and City Council controlled a number of these properties via tax sale certificates for years. Promises were made at that meeting, and we are diligently working with the Franklin Square community and COIL to develop a use for these properties. We do not think that it is unreasonable to ask that all owners of deteriorated properties be forced to abide by the housing code, including the City of Baltimore. There can simply be no discrimination in the enforcement of the housing code for Baltimore City. In fairness to Mayor Schmoke, I do not know how knowledgeable he is of this critical situation. I intend to invite him to view the adverse effect of DHCD's lack of uniform code enforcement and comprehensive planning. You as members will be notified.

Billie Fox

CHAPTER ELEVEN

Fast-forward – April 25, 2020

While I'm not the most adept person on a computer today, I decided to try to look up information on Mikal Abdullah and Mecca Construction to see if this company was still "in the game."

I was astonished to find a formal complaint (official report ID number 335287) had been filed with Ripoffs.com, alleging fraud. Intrigued, I decided to call the phone number listed, hoping to get some information on Mecca from the originators of the posting for my book. I was totally unaware that the individual who had made the complaint had posted the telephone number and address for one Mikal Abdullah, a contractor who obviously had corrupt ties to the minority no-bid program.

The man who answered the telephone did not identify himself but wanted to know the purpose of my call. I told him I was writing a book about fraud involving federal funds in Baltimore and Mecca Construction. He wanted to know the title of the book and publication date. He stated he was familiar with Mecca Construction and that I was incorrect about what had transpired in Baltimore. He stated there had been some indictments for bribery, but that Mecca was deemed to be "squeaky clean" by two FBI agents who came to meet with him regarding Mecca Construction. At no time did he identify himself as Mikal Abdullah. I told him the FBI agents I knew would never have used the term "squeaky clean" regarding Mecca Construction because they had seen the photo documentation of the properties awarded to the company in Baltimore, which were not renovated. He stated I was in error about the number of properties and dollar amounts. He further stated I was in error about the condition of the properties in March of 1995, when I attempted to testify at a government hearing calling for a city, state, and federal investigation. He cautioned me not to include this information in my book because I could be sued for slander. At this point, I told him not to try to threaten me, that this was America. I told him my civil rights were violated at the hearing in 1995 and that the truth about corruption in the no-bid contracts was going to be included. He stated Mecca was awarded five to six properties with renovation amounts of less than $40,000 per property. He stated all renovations were completed and that one property was expedited at the request of Mayor Schmoke.

I advised him once again that I definitely was not mistaken, because I was the individual who climbed into these vacant properties and took the photographs that were used to initiate an investigation, even though I was prevented from testifying in Baltimore City Council chambers. This person thought he could tell me I did not see or document what had been verified by the FBI. Obviously, there is a term for this type of thought process which makes individuals who prescribe this type of racial/religious ethos feel entitled and above the law.

Duplicity and funding requests for the same locations have been ignored by HUD for decades. One would think someone would have created an analytical computer program by now to "red-flag" these abuses. And there is absolutely no excuse for elected officials not reading funding requests and doing a physical inspection of the target areas. Imagine how stupid these elected officials must think their constituents are to keep voting them into office when nothing really changes but the dollars allocated are gone. The reality is these federal programs have been used to prop up insolvent urban areas—this simply has to stop. Capitalism will never work if local governments are allowed to mismanage federal funds while denying citizens access to stockpiled real estate basically being used for fraudulent activity.

President Trump was correct to call out Baltimore and Elijah Cummings for conditions in certain sections of the city, although it could have been a bit more tactful. There was no way Cummings could deny not being aware of abhorrent conditions. Over the years, he, too, was communicated with and shown the realities of mismanagement by DHCD and HUD. In fairness, there was little he could have done as one elected official to correct the nationwide abuse by so many cities, but there is no record that he ever brought these financial abuses to the attention of Congress. Once again, the situation existed even with someone as powerful as Cummings. It would have been political suicide to call out the Clinton administration or Obama administration for mismanagement by failing to demand accountability from all areas receiving federal assistance. Just think of how many middle-class do-gooders and up-lifters would be out of jobs if they actually administered programs correctly—every grant should be evaluated and terminated if it is not producing results.

In recent years, Baltimore had a program entitled "Vacants into Value," which was heralded by urban boosters as a success. In reality, many of the properties included in that program had already received funding and were not renovated by prior recipients of no-bid contracts like Mecca Construction. This also cannot be a black-and-white issue. It is a green issue only because it involves manipulating the economy to cover up monetary abuses.

In Baltimore, where properties have been placed in federal programs, HUD should allocate a specific amount of time for "their urban investment" to be brought into compliance with housing codes. The federal government could certainly seize those properties and mandate that they be sold to repay funds not properly used. Transparency in property transfers would quickly end the backroom deals in land disposition. Plus, there would be equal access if properly advertised. There should be an immediate moratorium on all real estate transactions involving M&CC-owned or controlled properties to ensure the assets of taxpayers are protected and the exact location of any federal funds appropriated to date.

Real estate manipulation in Baltimore by Joan Pratt, comptroller, appears to be finally being addressed by the inspector general's office. She was backed during her race for comptroller by powerful political and real estate developer State Senator Harry McGuirk back in 1994. Senator McGuirk indicated Pratt should be elected because that office controls the real estate and "that is where the money is."

The election of Joan Pratt was regarded as a victory for women, of sorts. Not only did she win the election against Senator Jack Lapides—"In Miss Pratt, we've [Baltimore] got a sugar mama"—according to Mike Littwin of the *Baltimore Sun*, commenting on her hiring of "Julius Henson, her [wink, wink] confidant and campaign manager/travel companion, a $79,000-a-year job, managing the city's multi-billion-dollar real estate holdings."

What a real estate game could be played deciding which property the feds would fund which year while owned by the city before selling or giving the titles (in the case of Bethel AME Church, fifteen for fifteen dollars—that's one dollar each) to private parties, who could then apply for funding. Hopefully, the federal auditors will do a forensic audit of funding in Baltimore with a "get-out-of-jail-free card" for employees who come forward.

Women of America, listen up! You had your shot in Baltimore and blew it—sometimes literally! Am I bad? It's time to shut up about gender and put qualified people in office just for the hell of it; vote male in Baltimore. Mayor Jack Young has given some stability to the city thus far, Bill Henry can certainly count, and with Kweisi Mfume or Kimberly Klacik in Congress, what can go wrong? Mfume restructured finances of the NAACP and was acutely aware of what transpired in Baltimore. How do I know? I stood on West Fayette Street years ago, outside of Morning Star Baptist Church, and detailed the scams going on while showing him the properties. I also called the NAACP when it was brought to my attention that some black professionals were victims of "shakedowns" during traffic stops. The officers allegedly would take their jewelry and cash, sometimes small amounts of pot, and let them slide. The receptionist at the NAACP that day must have thought she was auditioning for a Hollywood role as she told me in a phony, stilted white voice the NAACP did not involve itself in incidents where those complaining were violating the law. Then there was the issue of some select incarcerated voters having felonies downgraded to misdemeanors in order to get voter cards. I think Senator McGuirk would have supported the Kardashian-West team and their quest for sentencing justice. He was a political player, but most fair to constituents' needs, and believed that every vote counts. McGuirk would have supported sentencing justice which classifies many felonies as misdemeanors, thereby giving the accused the right to vote.

Americans have it within their power to end the cycle of abuse of federal funding. Rather than shy away from driving through less desirable neighborhoods, residents and visitors need to "tour" decayed areas with a pen and paper, or cell phone with a camera and video on.

Rather than nitpick their next-door neighbor about minor nuisances, residents need to embrace the boundaries of their cities and demand equity and enforcement of housing codes with total disregard for ownership. In Baltimore, properties owned or controlled by government agencies such as DHCD and hundreds of quasi-public entities were exempted from compliance with local housing laws. Homeowners and private investors were often hounded by inspectors and a legal process which totally ignored decaying properties connected with government entities.

HUD gives cities annual funding to maintain vacant properties. It was obvious these funds were being diverted in Baltimore, where properties were literally falling down. In some areas, dangling broken glass on upper floors to this date pose a threat to pedestrians.

As some neighborhoods went through revitalization, the slum properties locked into HUD programs continued to decay. Progressive officials at HUD were willing to consider allowing vacant, decaying properties in neighborhoods to be sold, providing another property was substituted; in so, the quota required under the original funding agreement was maintained.

The anonymous complaint filed against Mecca Construction really got me thinking about the whole Ponzi scheme/no-bid contract relationship. Many years have passed since the Bernie Madoff scandal, which was thoroughly investigated by the FBI after Andrew Madoff, the elder son, reported the fraud to federal authorities along with his younger brother, Mark. I called Jim Cabezas to tell him about my unpleasant conversation with the individual I presumed to be Mikal Abdullah on the phone. A "cyber sleuth" helping to verify data in my book traced the telephone number posted in the online complaint back to Mikal Abdullah in addition to the address listed. When I described the accusations against Mecca Construction, Mr. Cabezas said a "Ponzi scheme" was what it was called. That really got me thinking about the misguided no-bid contracts frequently awarded based solely on race—was this, and does it remain, an organized criminal conspiracy to defraud investors and the federal government? It would appear that this activity has gone on for decades and explains how companies like Mecca Construction went from state to state duping investors and leaving urban chaos behind. A check of corporate status in New Jersey, Maryland, and Georgia had shown Mecca in default years ago—no valid explanation as to how this company came to be involved in Baltimore HABC renovation funding could be offered by Arnold Jolivet, head of the Minority Contractors Association for decades. Someone in Baltimore would have had to provide information to Mecca Construction. That person or entity has never been identified. Another question that was never answered was whether Mikal Abdullah was a birth name or a name change because of conversion. It had been rumored that he was a relative of an elected official in Baltimore.

One of my confidants for years has been a former drug dealer who served his time, opened a business, founded a church, and is a truly outstanding human being with an amazing family. He explained to me that there are generally several reasons why black Americans change their names to African names. Sometimes the name change is for protection if someone is incarcerated—the Muslims protect their own in jails—and to ensure safety. Another reason is to hide relationships with public officials. Our parents sometimes don't know how to spell or think about how a name can impact a child when the formal name appears in print or is read aloud in school. Can you imagine why anyone would name a child "Frizzell" at birth? But this was the given name of one prominent legislator who later changed his name. Your guess is as good as mine.

It would be interesting to document how many inmates have changed their names during incarceration. Some people might say it is not constitutional to know the religious affiliation of public employees and elected officials, but the disclosure should be made if any action is being considered which would benefit these radical groups.

The relationship between the Nation of Islam and agencies granting federal funds needs close scrutiny. For decades, the impeccably dressed men in suits and bow ties have benefited financially from affiliation with elected officials. These purveyors of bean pies and racial hatred have gotten millions in benefits to provide housing for their members. They have operated successful programs in prisons which have radicalized generations of offenders. Moderates in the Muslim community have sought an inquiry into the practices of this radical group who were devout followers of Louis Farrakhan.

In Baltimore, HUD investigated DHCD when a no-bid contract was awarded to provide security in the infamous high-rise rental units operated by the Housing Authority of Baltimore City.

There was a sense of relief when the Schmoke administration left Baltimore. Corruption was rampant in the housing administration. The City of Baltimore had illegally exempted itself and other quasi-public entities from compliance with housing laws. Private owners were taken to court for violations on properties within view of properties owned or controlled by the City of Baltimore. Larry Chester, a building inspector who operated with integrity, wanted me to know he had nothing to do with signing off on permits showing that work had been completed on properties which were still in slum condition. It was Larry Chester who told me that Dan Henson had personally removed regular inspectors from the Mecca Construction project and assigned his own people. It was these individuals who falsified inspections which indicated work had been completed. The HUD inspectors were too lazy to get off their asses and physically inspect construction sites to ensure completion. Their negligence contributed to the filing of false grantee performance reports with the federal government. Nothing can be said to excuse the fact that local elected officials drove by these properties day after day and did nothing to call attention to the fraud. The media frequently refused to investigate allegations of funding abuse. There was wide coverage whenever HUD took on Baltimore, but not much journalistic investigation from the community perspective. The no-bid housing scandal could, and should, have been averted. HUD had taken on Baltimore when DHCD had violated federal guidelines. There was outrage over the decision of HUD to have competitive bidding.

The decision to sponsor a program to renovate vacant properties using the no-bid process was not a mistake but calculated corruption. Contractors were not properly vetted. Had there been an open bid process, the fraud involving well-connected minority contractors could have been prevented.

A network existed which allowed contractors of color with political connections to travel from city to city and state to state posing as legitimate minority contractors. There was justified outrage over the no-bid process, but no one wanted to step up and tell the truth—people were being awarded contracts based solely on the color of their skin with total disregard for their qualifications. The minority community was being sold out from within and the sellout was being tolerated.

It is assumed there is equity in America. The belief that we are created equal with inalienable rights is instilled from birth. Whenever an individual complains his civil rights have been violated, there is some individual or agency to ensure those rights are protected. In my case, there was no individual or agency who cared—at least none with the guts to stand up for a white community leader demanding accountability for the documented abuses of millions of dollars in federal funding. The failure to criminally charge individuals and agencies involved in the fraud still makes no sense. What makes even less sense is the role the Clinton White House played in ending the FBI investigation into the fraud and corruption in Baltimore City.

It made no sense for Daniel P. Henson, a.k.a. "Dirty Dan," to be selected to coordinate housing development in Africa. After all, this was the man who removed qualified inspectors, assigned to inspect properties allegedly being renovated by Mecca Construction, and replaced them with incompetent flunkies who would sign off on anything per Henson's orders. Mecca should never had been paid for renovating properties which were in slum condition when permits were falsified. Rather than being investigated and prosecuted for corruption in Baltimore, Henson was rewarded by the Clinton Foundation when he teamed up with a member of the affluent Mitchell family to oversee the development of housing in Africa.

The Department of Housing and Community Development was left in shambles with the retirement of Henson. There was no smooth transition—the chatter of the day was gossip over the blank computer screens left in the department.

It is laughable to read the biography of the Henson Development Company on the internet today. What a scam and what a shame. I would recommend anyone considering this firm drive through Baltimore, Maryland, to do a reality check and also check out the prevalent fraud in the housing development in Africa.

For decades, many elected officials have known about what could be called the domestic deficit. It is easy to understand the frantic verbiage of legislators whose actions the past few decades led to defrauding the federal government of billions of dollars. The game plan was so very simple: use the federal block grant program to access funds which would be diverted to cover budget deficits. It was correctly assumed federal employees would honor as accurate false grantee performance reports, indicating the funds had been used for the stated purpose.

Rather than worry about who will win or lose the next election, elected officials need to come clean with the American electorate now. There are many elected officials who have remained silent, knowing their colleagues generally can't figure out what is going on. It is these individuals who should be indicted for their silence on the runaway domestic deficit resulting from decades of fraudulent block grant applications.

If President Trump were to order all cities and states getting any federal funds to submit an annual financial statement, it would reveal the true financial status of many cities desperate for funding due to prior mismanagement.

There has been too much crotch intrigue and too little monitoring of what has been happening to the physical and financial infrastructure of America.

Hopefully, Donald Trump will order a forensic accounting for federal block grant monies allocated and not used for the stated purpose. Elected officials on all levels of government should be held accountable for any false grantee performance report submitted. Employees within agencies who falsified any documents cannot be given leniency, nor should HUD employees who process documents containing misrepresentations be exonerated. Committee chairpersons in Congress should be removed and replaced immediately if corruption took place during their tenure.

Perhaps it is time for a swamp rescue. Extend an olive branch of amnesty to those municipalities in a financial crisis because of past abuses. Be prepared for some to choose going down the drain by not opting to come clean and become part of a stronger nation.

Say it any way you'd like, *LES JEUX SONT FAITS*, the games have ended.

We are not a country of bigots, racists, and idiots as portrayed by many. We have the capability to come forward and unite with purpose.

The decision to attend the city council hearing involving the no-bid housing project was not easy. I had met privately with almost every member of the Baltimore City Council, state legislators, and congressional representatives, and many of them had read the contents of my infamous Red Envelope. The envelope contained adequate proof of fraud involving almost every level of the process. The contents remain confidential.

BIBLIOGRAPHY

Camp, Patricia. "Shopsteading for City Neighborhoods." *Washington Post*, 1978.

Daemmrich, JoAnna. "Council to probe city repairs." *Baltimore Sun*, 1995.

Defilippo, Frank A. "Housing: the Henson family follies." *Baltimore Business Journal*, 1997.

Dr. Albert O. Kuhn, letter in regard to H. L. Mencken House. December 18, 1973.

Edney, Hazel Trice. "Sharpton Backs Away from Car Loans Commercials." BlackVoiceNews.com, 2005.

Fox, Billie. "President's Message." *Union Square Bulletin*, 1990.

Higham, Scott, and Melody Simmons. "HUD demands $725,759 from city." *Baltimore Sun*, 1995.

Higham, Scott, Marcia Myers, Melody Simmons, and Norris P. West. "Keeping secrets from Uncle Sam." *Baltimore Sun*, 1995.

Kurt L. Schmoke, letter from Ardebella Fox. July 15, 1994.

Littwin, Mike. "What Joan Pratt has done for women should make men feel a lot less sleazy." *Baltimore Sun*, 1996.

McCarthy, Andrew C. "Law + The Courts – The President's Power to End a Criminal Investigation." National Review.com, 2017.

Myers, Marcia, and JoAnna Daemmrich. "Few questions, fewer answers at hearing on housing repairs." *Baltimore Sun*, 1995.

Olesker, Michael. "Housing issues ruled out of order at Hall's Hearing." *Baltimore Sun*, 1995.

Robert Embry, letter in regard to H. L. Mencken House. November 4, 1975.

Rogan, Tom. "Reverend-huckster Al Sharpton smells a Charlottesville profit." *Washington Examiner*, 2017.

Ronald Miles, letter from the author. February 15, 1991.

Shesgreen, Deirdre, and Van Smith. "Top Ten Our Writers' Picks for 1995." *City Paper*, 1995.

William Donald Schaefer, letter in regard to H. L. Mencken House. March 10, 1977.

CPSIA information can be obtained
at www.ICGtesting.com
Printed in the USA
LVHW052238080321
680888LV00016B/3143